Surviving Abuse

A Journey to Forgiveness and Freedom .

Marie Cook

Blessings
to you!
Marie Cook

TATE PUBLISHING & Enterprises

Published by Tate Publishing & Enterprises, LLC
127 E. Trade Center Terrace | Mustang, Oklahoma 73064 USA
1.888.361.9473 | www.tatepublishing.com

Tate Publishing is committed to excellence in the publishing industry. The company reflects the philosophy established by the founders, based on Psalm 68:11,
"The Lord gave the word and great was the company of those who published it."

Book design copyright © 2010 by Tate Publishing, LLC. All rights reserved.
Cover design by Scott Parrish
Interior design by Blake Brasor

Published in the United States of America

ISBN: 978-1-61739-010-4
1. Religion, Christian Life, Inspirational
2. Family & Relationships, Abuse, General
10.08.05

Dedication

This book is dedicated to my husband, who stood by me and supported me in everything I have lived through, loving me through my tears, triumphs, and tragedies.

This book is also dedicated to my Nanny, who was always proud of me, loved me unconditionally, and believed in me when I didn't believe in myself.

Acknowledgments

I want to thank my husband for standing by me. He has been there to shoulder my pain and anguish, has helped me pick up the pieces of a broken shattered heart, and has given me more encouragement, support, and love than I could ever imagine. He helps me laugh through the toughest of times and helps me to see a little humor in everything. I love you with all my heart; you are my best friend and my life partner.

I want to thank my counselor and friend, Joanna. I love you! Thank you for the gift of letting go, for the ability to work through the pain, and for allowing me to come to the truth when I didn't want to see it.

I want to thank the ladies in my growth groups who saw me cry and did not judge me; thank you for sharing your stories with me and allowing me to learn that I was not alone in what I suffered.

Finally, I want to thank a pastor who was placed in my life at the right time, Pastor Jim. Pastor Jim has since gone on to be with the Lord, and I miss him very much. He confirmed God's grace and love in my life. He gave me hope and courage that God indeed loves me and wants what is best for me. He helped me discern biblical passages and allowed me to learn the truth of God's Word.

Table of Contents

Introduction

I want to start out by stating that I am not a professor, nor do I have a degree. This book is written through experience and at the direction of the Holy Spirit living in me. This book contains my personal views and opinions unless otherwise noted. All scripture is taken from *The Quest Bible Study* (NIV).

When God planted the seed in my mind about writing this book, I started in with all the excuses, like Moses, for why I am not qualified to write this book. The Almighty graciously, lovingly, and patiently reminded me that many of the people who wrote parts of the Bible did not have a college degree either. Saint Paul wrote a quarter of the Bible while in chains and in prison. If you take a look at history in the Bible, you will see that God almost always uses the weak and helpless to do great things for Him and His kingdom.

This book is not just for you, but it is also a healing tool for me. I will be opening myself up to you, a stranger, in the hope that through my experience you will be encouraged to forgive the people who have hurt you. This book is not meant to focus on my abuse or point fingers at the abusers; however, this book will paint a picture of abuse, the devastating effects it has on people, and, most importantly, the healing power of forgiveness through our Lord and Savior, Jesus Christ.

I would strongly suggest that you read one chapter at a time, absorbing the contents, the Scripture passages, and truthfully answer the questions at the end of each chapter. Ponder your thoughts, write down your hurts, and give them to God, the Great Healer. This book is written to give all the glory to God the Father, Jesus Christ, His Son, and the Holy Spirit. I am a simple humble servant called to glorify Jesus Christ and His awesome love and forgiveness through His healing power and redemption. I was once very lost, but now I am found!

―――――――

I wrote this book for me—not you—to help heal the wounds that have deeply scarred me. The Holy Spirit prompted and directed me. However, if you are reading this book, then I sincerely hope that it will help you as well. Through God's Holy Word, I have allowed God to heal my shattered broken heart, cleanse and bandage the wounds with His love, and I have given all of the pain, anger, rage, hatred, and all other negative emotions to God that I carried around for so many years.

My greatest prayer and hope is that it will help others who have deep wounds from abuse. If you are reading this book, chances are that you have been wounded and abused. I am sorry that you had to go through that pain. My heart goes out to you. Let me tell you one thing I know for sure: God never intended for you or me to suffer abuse. He loves us with a great unconditional love that cannot be measured, comprehended, or understood fully until we meet with our glorious Lord and Savior, Jesus Christ, face to face.

If you are not a believer in Jesus, my greatest prayer would be for you to come to the cross, accept the free gift of salvation, and lay down your sins, transgressions, hurts, wounds, and pain and allow the Great Healer to heal and restore you. You will never fill that void in the very center of your being with anything else that will satisfy. Jesus is the answer.

The focus of this book is to show how, through forgiveness, we can be free of all the negative emotions and feelings that surround abuse. I did not write this book to point fingers and prove how mean and rotten my abuser has been. I did not write this book to have my abuser persecuted or condemned. My focus and reason for writing this book is to focus on forgiveness and the healing power of Christ. Throughout the book, I do share my abuse and open my heart and life to all who read it; however, you will not find the real names that would lead you to figure out who my abuser is by name. That is not my intent. God will deal with my abuser in His time and in His justice, not mine. I want you to hear my heart on this, beloved. I wish no harm or ill upon my abuser. In fact, through Christ, I have even come to love the very person who inflicted all of the pain upon my brother and me.

For any family member who reads this book, you will know whom I am talking about. I simply can't help that and have taken as many precautions as I can to ensure the anonymity of my abuser. I have to love her from afar, and I have to allow Christ to love her through me, but I can say that I do love her, and I do pray for her on a regular basis. I pray that God would open her eyes and help her to heal from her abuse.

My abuser was abused. That is part of the cycle of generational sin. I will talk about generational sin in "Sins of Omission and Generational Sin Equals Abuse" of this book. So you see, I can't really hold anything against her because she was a victim, too, as are most abusers, and I would venture to say the person who abused you was as well. People who have been abused tend to lash out at the weak and helpless in an attempt to control their own pain and abuse issues. I saw this with my abuser, and I myself started down that path as well.

That is, until God got my attention and said that through me He would end the generational sin of abuse in my family. Unfortunately, it has cost me my entire family, whom I love dearly, but my experience and ability to live freely in Christ is what I gained. I continue to pray for my family and ask God to reconcile us one to the other. I trust that God will bring them, one by one, into a deep and everlasting relationship with the King of kings and Lord of lords, Jesus Christ. If I can't enjoy my family on this earth, then my fervent prayer and deepest hope would be to spend eternity with them in a loving kingdom with Christ at the center of everything, like He intended from the beginning.

When you read my story, you may get angry. That is okay. My story may remind you of the abuse in your life and may cause you to become angry and bitter against the person or persons who abused you. I would urge you to give these feelings to God and completely surrender them to Him. Don't hang on to the negative feelings; they will only hurt you and not your abuser.

It is so like our human nature to want to take revenge, to get back and hurt the person who hurt us so deeply. I know; I was there. Believe me; God can bring about situations that are far more justifying than any scheme or plan you could come up with to retaliate against your abuser. Forgive; hand God all of your negative feelings and emotions and your revenge; step out of His way and live! You will be set free from those bonds and chains. God is no respecter of persons, and He can and will do for you what He has done for me. I am just a humble servant who has been set free.

Jesus said and Paul quotes in Romans 15:2b, "The insults of those who insult you have fallen on me."

Jesus took your sin, your hurt and pain with Him to the cross. He died for you, and He loves you today. He was raised from death three days after dying on the cross. Do you know what that means? It means that you can have total and complete freedom and salvation in the only Son of God, Jesus Christ! Forgiveness heals. Jesus heals and cleanses wounds to set you free.

All of the references to satan have purposely been left uncapitalized and are not typos. I absolutely refuse to give any type of respect or grammatical correctness to the evil one of this world and so have chosen to not capitalize his name or show any type of respect to him in that way. By way of contrast, all of the references to God, Jesus Christ, and the Holy Spirit are capitalized.

I would like to end this introduction with a prayer for you and for me:

Father God, the one who is reading this book, in all probability, has been abused by someone. You know this person, Father, and you know his or her wounds. You see his or her pain and hurt, and I would just ask You now that You would do for this person what you have done for me. Please set him or her free; cleanse his or her wounds, heal his or her heart, and help this person to forgive completely those who have wounded and abused him or her. Father, you are the Great Healer. You sent Your only Son not to condemn this world but to save all people through Your mercy, love, and grace. Show Your love to this person in a powerful way and help him or her in his or her journey to forgive those who have wounded him or her. Give him or her the strength to face the truth of his or her abuse; help him or her, Father, to then pray for the person who abused him or her. I ask all of this in Jesus's name. Amen.

Child Abuse:

The Beginning of My Journey

And whoever welcomes a little child like this in My name welcomes Me. But if anyone causes one of these little ones who believe in Me to sin, it would be better for him to have a large millstone hung around his neck and to be drowned in the depths of the sea. Woe to the world because of the things that cause people to sin! Such things must come, but woe to the man through whom they come!

Matthew 18:5–7

A little girl of seven years of age hides, shaking with fear in her room, rocking back and forth on her bed crying at the sound of pain and anguish coming from her brother's room; she hears statements like, "You stay in that room, little girl, or you will get it even worse!"

The little girl yells back, "I'm going to tell Daddy! I hate you! I hate you!"

The mother replies with, "You go right ahead and tell your father and see what happens to you."

The little girl feels the helplessness of her situation; she feels that she has let her brother down, that she has failed to protect him. These beatings of her brother happened on a daily basis, and the beatings she sustained came at least twice a week and sometimes more. All this little seven-year-old child can think to do is cry and rock and try to find some way to block the horrible events that penetrated her very being and soul. The horrible, ugly fact that her brother is being beaten yet again with a belt across his bare skin by their mother is too much for this child to bear, and so the memory blocking process begins.

That little girl was me. The events of the past are true, very real, and this is my story.

It didn't always used to be that way. We used to live in the suburbs of Detroit, Michigan, until I was seven years old; my brother was five. My father was transferred to a job some 250 miles north of Detroit. I remember good times with family and friends. I remember going to a school where large jungle animals were painted on the walls. I remember spending time with my grandparents, aunts, uncles, and cousins. Life was wonderful, and there was no abuse.

After moving north, things changed drastically. I remember clearly driving into the town that would become our home and feeling this ugly black sense that there was something not right about that place. I couldn't put my finger on it, but young as I was, I knew there was something in this town that was evil. I am not the only one who has felt this way about the town I grew up in. A dear friend of mine moved to this town from another state, and she stated that she felt the same dark ugly presence hovering over the town but couldn't quite figure out what or why this seemed to be. If you come to this town, you will feel the very same ugly negative presence as you walk through the public buildings and through town. Guaranteed, you will not be able to figure out the strange black feeling, but you will definitely be able to sense something is not quite right there.

Our extended family was down state, and we were secluded from everything and everyone we once knew. My father went to work almost immediately, and my mother stayed at home. My mother began to change. She started yelling and became nasty toward us. Then the beatings started. We would get beat with belts, wooden spoons, and her hands. The reasons for the beatings were because we didn't clean the bathroom properly, we weren't quiet during her soap operas, or we supposedly talked back to her.

Mind you, I was seven and my brother was five years old. We were children! To this day, I cannot clean bathrooms, floors, appliances, or vacuum without horrible memories flooding my mind. My wonderful husband does the cleaning or we hire it out.

My brother and I were expected to act like adults when we didn't know what that meant. The physical abuse I sustained lasted until I was fourteen. I can't honestly remember when it stopped for my brother. I believe it stopped when he started hitting back.

My brother reports an incident where he claims that my mother actually tried to kill me by pushing my face into a pillow and whipping me with a belt. I remember waking up in my bed but couldn't remember how I got there. My brother stated that he literally had to pull my three-hundred-pound mother off me, and when he turned me over, my face was blue. He said that she made a statement to him that the only reason she gave me mouth-to-mouth resuscitation was because she couldn't find a good enough reason to explain to our father why his daughter was dead. I don't have much memory of that incident, but that doesn't mean it didn't happen. I was seven when the alleged incident happened.

Today, some thirty-plus years later, the unblocked memories bring stinging tears to my eyes, and I can still feel a shadow of the hopelessness, fear, and confusion the abuse generated back then. Through the grace of God, I want to share with you how I was able to not only forgive my mother and father, but how I am now able to allow Christ to love them through me, pray for them, and lay to rest all thoughts of revenge, hatred, rage, and anger. God is a very powerful healer, and if we allow Him into our shattered broken hearts, He can and will heal us.

The questions that ran through my head as a child haunted me to adulthood. Questions like, *Why was I born? Why did my mother hate me all of sudden? What terrible crime had we done to warrant being beaten? Why didn't my earthly father protect us or ever question my mother as to why the children were always in their rooms when he came home?* Job 3:11–13 captured my feelings perfectly: "Why did I not perish at birth and die as I came from the womb? Why were there knees to receive me and breasts that I might be nursed? For now I would be lying down in peace; I would be asleep and at rest."

My subconscious mind took over and started blocking most of the memories of abuse I sustained as a child. However, not all of the memories were blocked. I remembered bits and pieces of abuse. I remembered yelling at my mother that I hated her. I can still feel the shadow of that hate. Thank God the Holy Spirit lives within me and has removed the real hate, rage, and anger that existed for so long. There are moments, even today, when an unblocked memory will surface and I have to relive it, go through it, forgive, and hand it over to God for Him to deal with.

Ironically, my parents professed a faith in Jesus Christ, forced us to go to church, join a Kids' Club at church, and did all the "right" things that looked good on the outside. I use the word *forced* because that is exactly what it was—force. My brother and I did not want any part of church. To us, it was a social club to see who was wearing the latest fashion, who had the best behaved children, and a place where adults could talk with other adults.

They kept talking about a God, but I didn't know who that was or even if I wanted to know who this God was. We were not sure why it was important to go to church, because going to church didn't change my parents' behavior during the week. Starting Monday, we were beaten mercilessly, given the drug Ritalin so our mother could watch her soap operas in peace and quiet, and were ordered to play outside without adult supervision. During the week, I did not observe my parents reading the Bible or praying. God was rarely talked about except on Sundays and then we were encouraged to pray to Him as our Father. Who? Our Father? Where was He? How come we couldn't see Him, and if He claimed to love us, why didn't He rescue us when we were being beaten?

We already had a father, but he was too busy for us. My father usually worked six days a week, and when he was home, he had more important things to do, such as mow the grass or work on projects without the children around. As most children do, I compared God the Father to my earthly mother and father. If this God was anything like my parents, I honestly didn't want any part of Him or It or whatever was up there beyond the stars. Besides, my mother told me if I had sex before getting married, I would go to hell; if I disobeyed my parents, I would go to hell; if I didn't get good grades ... well, you get the idea. Since I had already broken most of those rules, what was the point? I was going to hell anyway, so I might as well enjoy the ride while I was still on this earth. Ah, the wages of sin—it is death and it does lead to destruction, as I would soon find out.

I want to get back to playing outside without adult supervision and the impact and damage that had on both my brother and me. We had several kids to play with in our neighborhood, but there was this older kid named Clyde, and he was abused by his father, a fact I didn't learn about until much later in life. Clyde sexually abused the younger neighborhood boys down in the woods. Unfortunately, my brother was one of his victims.

I remember one hot day in July when I was riding my bike down the path that led to the woods. I had to get my brother as Mom was preparing lunch for us between the commercials of her soap operas. When I found my brother, a very strange and weird feeling came over me. I knew something was very wrong. Clyde started walking toward me and laughed as he said, "Maybe we should give her a checkup like you guys have had."

Something in me welled up and propelled me to jump on my bike and ride as fast as I could back up the hill toward home. Clyde was chasing me, and I was screaming at the top of my lungs. No one came out to find out why I was screaming. When I got home and told my mother, she dismissed it as boys just playing around. I don't know how long my brother was sexually abused, nor do I know the extent of that abuse. I know it has affected his life severely, and I have seen the pain in his eyes. If my mother had paid more attention, if she had been watchful of her children, if ... if only. This is another form of sin: the omission. There should always be adult supervision around when older children are present with younger children.

My mother had a way of making me feel completely inadequate. My grades were never good enough; my friends were never good enough; nothing I ever did or said was good enough. She had a way (which continues to this day) of taking God's Word out of context and applying it to her own agenda to make herself look good and right. For instance, "Honor your father and your mother, so that you may live long in the land the Lord your God is giving you" (Exodus 20:12).

My mother so ingrained into our heads that this verse meant we were to do everything she told us to do without question, and if we questioned her, we were not honoring her. I struggled for years with this passage of Scripture, and it wasn't until years later I truly understood the true meaning and could put to rest the lie that had been so ingrained in me.

Another example was that she would state she was saved by Jesus Christ and she could do whatever she wanted to do, and it was okay in God's eyes because she was saved. She explained to us that when we received Jesus as our Lord and Savior that He forgave all of our sins—past, present and future—so it was okay to continue sinning knowing that we were saved and would go to heaven no matter what we did. That is *not* what the Bible teaches; however, she continues to live this lie even today.

Colossians 3:5, 8–10 states:

> For you died, and your life is now hidden with Christ in God (*you accept Jesus Christ as your Lord and Savior–you have died to your old self*). When Christ, who is your life, appears then you also will appear with him in glory. Put to death, therefore, whatever belongs to your early nature: sexual immorality, impurity, lust, evil desires and greed, which is idolatry. But now you must rid yourselves of all such things as these: anger, rage, malice, slander,

and filthy language from your lips. Do not lie to each other, since you have taken off your old self with its practices and have put on the new self, which is being renewed in knowledge in the image of its Creator.

The reality is that once you accept Jesus as your Lord and Savior, you are to put off your old sinful ways of doing things and be renewed and transformed into the image of Christ. This doesn't happen overnight, and we are all prone to fail, but to continue to live purposefully in sin is not right and that is what my mother has done and continues to do and, unfortunately, believes she can do as she pleases without consequences and believing that all she does is covered under the blood of Christ without further judgment from Him.

Finally, the third way I remember her taking Scripture out of context was that she continually says we are not to judge her. Only God can judge, and we are never to question anything she says or does. However, Matthew 18:15–17 states:

If your brother sins against you, go and show him his fault, just between the two of you. If he listens to you, you have won your brother over. But if he will not listen, take one or two others along so that every matter may be established by the testimony of two or three witnesses. If he refuses to listen to them, tell it to the church and if he refuses to listen even to the church, treat him as you would a pagan or a tax collector.

The mental and spiritual abuse was more horrific than the physical abuse. We were not allowed to cry as children. When my mother was beating us, she ordered us not to cry or we would get caught in a vicious cycle of crying and beating. How can you tell your children not to cry when they are suffering physical pain?

For many years, I had a very hard time crying in front of anyone, and I am still battling that to this day. I remember the first time I cried in front of my husband. It took a lot of trust, and his love overwhelmed me as the sobbing and shaking continued until my body was a limp noodle, and I was drained. God is working on me, and I hope to someday not have any fear of crying in front of anyone.

Mental humiliation was a big part of my mother's control and manipulation of us. I remember when my mother told me about the "birds and the bees." She told me about women going through a menstrual cycle but never really explained what that meant. "It is just something a woman goes though" is an example of some of the words she would say.

One day I got my period. I was fifteen, and I had no idea what was happening to me. I literally thought I was dying, as blood was coming out of my body for no apparent reason. I raced down to the laundry room and asked my mother what was happening. When she saw my fear, the tears, and heard me say that I thought I was dying, she laughed. She found humor in my distress and fear. She then explained what was happening with my body and that I was not dying. I pleaded with her not to tell Daddy or my brother, as this was terribly embarrassing for me.

Later that evening, around the dinner table, my mother said in a very demeaning and loud voice, "Guess who became a woman today?" and proceeded to tell my father and brother that I had started my period, and then she laughed as she recalled my fear and tears about dying. I was mortified! I got up and ran to my bedroom, so embarrassed and distressed that I grabbed what clothes I could, throwing them into a backpack and ran out of the house, jumped on my bike, and headed for my grandmother's home.

My mother didn't stop there. She would reiterate the entire humiliating story to her friends and people at church, not keeping it in the family. It got to be so embarrassing that I developed a complex and felt that everyone knew what had happened to me. This wasn't a simple humorous story; she would maliciously embarrass me if we saw someone she knew in a store or out in public. She made it a point to embarrass me at every turn and didn't care how many men were around to hear it. The humiliation I suffered followed me into adulthood, and it played a negative role when I got married to my husband. I constantly felt dirty and ashamed when that time of the month came around. I didn't sleep much during that week as I was scared to death of having any type of accident in bed. I didn't want my husband to look upon me as unclean, nor did I want him to think any less of me.

This is the kind of mental abuse and humiliation that was commonplace in our home.

When I was of age to drive, I started going out a lot—anything to get out of the house and away from my mother. The physical abuse had stopped for the most part, save for the occasional strike to the face, but the mental, emotional, and spiritual abuse had just begun. I would go to a dance club with my girlfriends, drive around town, date many guys, and do anything and everything that would keep me away from home.

I graduated from high school and had no clue as to what I wanted to do with my life. I was very much afraid of my mother and dared not cross her lest I find my face on the floor. I was looking for a way out. I would take the first chance I got to move out of the house. I would soon get my chance.

At this point, I think it is very important for you to realize that the abuse that I sustained and went through turned itself into rebellion and a severe hatred toward all people and even to God. I trusted no one, hated my mother, but loved my father, brother, grandmother, and extended family. I didn't have many friends, as I was afraid to get close to anyone. I acted out and had unhealthy relationships with men in a desperate attempt to find true love, happiness, and most of all, protection. All of these relationships led to heartache and more pain. I was on the wrong track. Through the grace of God alone, I did not end up with a child out of wedlock. I am not an alcoholic, nor am I a drug addict, and I didn't obtain any kind of sexually transmitted disease. Praise God for His faithfulness, patience, protection, and incredible love!

There was a woman in my life that became my best friend and gave me a glimpse of what God was really like. That woman was my grandmother, my father's mother. I loved her dearly. She was my safe haven, my refuge, and my protector. When I was old enough, I could ride my bike the seven miles to her house and stay safe. She taught me about unconditional love, and, looking back, showed me how to forgive.

God places people like this in your life for a reason. For me, it showed me that there was someone out there who cared about me, loved me, and didn't expect me to be perfect. My grandmother modeled for me the unconditional love of Christ, a lesson I didn't learn or understand until much later in life. My grandmother died when I was eighteen. I lost my best friend, my protector, and my confidante. My world crashed in upon me, and I fell into a deep pit that was mired with pain and anger.

I was dealing with incredible pain, and I couldn't imagine my world without my grandmother. Who would protect me? Who would console me? So many questions, my head swam. I was looking for a way out and fast. My mother was unstable at best, and my father was totally disconnected emotionally. In fact, my father did not even cry at his own mother's funeral!

About two months after Grandma's funeral, I went out one evening with a girlfriend and we went to a dance club. She had a boyfriend who had a good buddy. I was not seeing anyone in particular at that time and neither was the good buddy. Needless to say, we were introduced, and I found my way out. We started going out and seeing each other quite a bit. He had just moved into a bachelor pad, and it just so happened that one of the guys was moving out to attend a college down state. It was September; my parents went on vacation farther north, leaving my ninety-something-year-old grandfather at home alone with my brother and me.

You have to understand that this was a time in my life when I had lost my best friend and protector in the form of my grandmother (my father's mother). She died in a hospital of cardiac arrest, and when she died, my whole world fell apart. I wanted nothing to do with God. I was so angry at Him for taking her away from me that I went into a rebellious mode. I lived in reckless abandon and didn't care if I lived or died. I met my future husband during this time. I was under the false belief that if I gave myself to a man that he would love, care for, and protect me. I want to clarify something here: I did not sleep around with every Tom, Dick, and Harry that came along. I was very selective of my partners and only had relationships with those I thought I was in love with and with those who I believed loved me.

When I met my future husband, we started dating. The time had come, I thought, when we should take our relationship to the next level. Even though he was not a Christian and had no knowledge of faith or Jesus, he resisted my sexual advances. I was shocked! No other guy had resisted me. After all, I was very pretty, slender, and had a knockout body—if I do say so myself. Not only did he resist my sexual advances, but he did not force himself on me or try to get me into bed. This guy truly was different from the other guys I had dated.

This guy was indeed different, and I liked him very much. We were both getting over previous relationships and were literally floundering when we were introduced. I knew the second I met him that he would become my husband. It wasn't long after we started dating that I moved in with my future husband and we began a life together.

I decided, at age nineteen, to leave home for good. I packed my belongings, and with the help of my new boyfriend (who would eventually become my husband) and his pals, we proceeded to move me out of my parents' home and into his apartment. I had two cats, and they were going to move in with me. I told my then-boyfriend, "Take me, take my cats; don't take my cats, I'm gone." So the cats and I moved in. I left my parents a note on the table telling them I had moved out. I chose to move out when they were gone because I was deathly afraid of my mother's wrath and literally feared for my life.

After I moved, my mother kept in touch with me. I tried to avoid her at every turn, because she never had a positive thing to say to me or about my life. Everything was negative and there was no support.

The emotional abuse continued. I had intense fear and dread toward my mother but didn't have all of the unblocked memories to fully comprehend or understand why.

Let's fast forward to a young woman of twenty-two who is about to get married to a man she dearly loves. My soon-to-be husband and I had lived together for three years and decided it was time to become "legal." We realized we could receive better tax breaks and decided that we wanted to spend the rest of our lives together. Matthew loved me dearly, never laid an ugly hand on me, and became my best friend. He cared for me, loved me, but most of all, he provided a sense of protection for me.

Strangely enough, about a month prior to the wedding, horrible and horrific memories came flooding back. I mean really ugly visions and memories of my mother beating me, my brother, and the family dog. What was all this? Was I going crazy? Was I hallucinating? Thankfully, I worked for a psychotherapist at the time. One of the memories that came back was of a time when my mother went out and beat our family pet, a Newfoundland dog, for barking. She locked the dog in the garage and took a broom to her. I remembered listening to the animal cry out in pain as if begging my mother to stop. As this memory came flooding back, I sat at my desk. The pain, fear, and helplessness was overpowering and I went into my boss's office crying, shut her door, and proceeded to ask for help. I thought I was going crazy.

My boss explained that, no, I wasn't going crazy. I had been abused and my mind had blocked memories too powerful and painful for my conscious mind to absorb, handle, and deal with. "But why now?" I asked, "Why now, one month before getting married?" It was explained to me that my subconscious mind felt safe to reveal the memories I had blocked as a child and was now allowing my conscious mind to relive the truth in an attempt to handle and deal with the pain, anger, rage, and horror of the reality of this abuse. What I didn't realize at the time was that God was allowing these memories to come back so that He could lead me through the pain, anger, rage, and hate that I felt for my mother.

You see, you have to go through the pain, anger, rage, and hate. You can't go around it; you can't go over it; you can't keep it down inside you forever because it always finds a way out, and you can't go under it in an attempt to sweep it all under the rug. You have to go through it. Relive the pain and memories, forgive those who inflicted this abuse upon you, and then hand them over to Jesus. Please hear me on this. Jesus asks us to forgive, and He will help you to forget. I think initially He allows us to remember the painful memories of abuse so we can learn and not pass them on. However, as we shall explore, sometimes the sins of the parents get passed on to the next generation.

> You shall not bow down to them or worship them; for I, the LORD your God, am a jealous God, punishing the children for the sin of the fathers to the third and fourth generation of those who hate me, but showing love to a thousand generations of those who love me and keep my commandments.
>
> Exodus 20:5–6

I met with my boss for counseling sessions, sometimes two or three times a week. She didn't dock my paycheck or charge me for her services. I was able to work through the immediate memories that began to unblock but still had many questions. After dealing with these memories, I thought all of the abuse issues were behind me even though I didn't have answers to everything, but I thought I was ready to move forward with my life as a married woman. Besides, I rationalized that once I was married, my husband would protect me, and we could live our life on our own terms as a married couple and not under the thumb of my mother any longer.

I still had many questions that neither I nor my boss could answer. I didn't understand why my subconscious mind had to bring these memories back to my conscious, and I definitely didn't want to relive that part of my past. But God had other plans. I would have to undergo more counseling years later to really get to the root issues that I was struggling with.

My mother continued to try to control every aspect of my life, and many of the wedding plans and decisions were made by her without much input from us even though we tried to input our decisions, feelings, desires, and wants. There were times when Matthew and I almost eloped because my mother's plans and requests were overbearing for us. It got to be so intense that we almost threw in the towel and broke up before we were married. We wanted a very simple and straightforward wedding without a lot of hoopla, glitz, and glamour. My mother wanted a wedding not for her daughter but to show off herself and to appear that she spared no expense. This wedding turned out to be "the social gathering of the year" for my mother and had really nothing to do with me. It was all about glitz and glam and "look at me; look at me and what I have done and accomplished." She really never took into consideration our requests, thoughts, feelings, or how we wanted things done. It was all about her and how she looked and appeared to the masses.

We ended up getting married three years after we starting dating and are still together today, some twenty-plus years later!

This chapter ends the childhood portion of my life.

Does any of this sound familiar to you? Maybe you weren't abused like this, but has someone in your life hurt you physically, emotionally, spiritually, or sexually? Abuse is abuse is abuse. It all leaves the same ugly effects of depression, despair, hopelessness, fear, anger, hate, rage, and the need for justification and/or revenge. You can get rid of all of that negative emotional baggage when you place your faith in Jesus Christ and when you allow Him to come in and heal your wounds.

Let's review the facts:

1. I was physically, mentally, emotionally, and spiritually abused by my mother. The sins of my father were those of omission—turning the blind eye and looking the other way.

2. I took on this abuse as my fault and blamed myself for some unknown sin that I had committed. If I could have been good or perfect, smart enough, or strong enough, then maybe the abuse would stop. The truth is, I was a child and I was in no way to blame for this abuse. There is no justification for child abuse.

3. I didn't want anything to do with a God that allowed children to be abused and hurt. I blamed Him for this abuse and wrongfully rationalized that if this is how God operates, I didn't want anything to do with Him. We must realize that there is evil in this world and that evil is called satan. The evil one cajoles and tempts us into committing sin.

4. I tried to escape the pain and abuse and attempted to find love my own way through wrong relationships. What I really needed was God. He is the only One that can truly heal us from wounds that have cut us so very deep. When your soul has been pierced, your spirit crushed, and you want to die rather than live; He is the only One that can heal that kind of wound and pain. Trust me; I am speaking from experience here.

5. At this point, I was married, working, and trying to deal with the unblocked memories of my past all by myself and it wasn't working.

Questions to Ponder

Now, take a look at your life and your past. Ask yourself the following questions, ponder them for a moment, and even write down your thoughts. Release your answers to God through the prayer below. One step at a time, one layer at a time, let's peel back the hurt and pain that is covering up the real you.

1. Has there been someone in your life that has hurt you deeply? If so, name that person and the circumstances that surround the pain and hurt. This doesn't have to be just child abuse. This can be a relationship where you were not treated right, a spouse who just dumped you and left you to survive alone. Could it be someone who has taken advantage of you financially, physically, or emotionally? Was it someone you worked for? Was it a family member that broke your trust or a trusted friend who broke your confidence? Who hurt you? Write down the name or names and a brief explanation of the circumstances.

   _____

   _____

   _____

2. How do you feel about that person? Is there anger, hate, and/or rage coursing through your blood and

veins? Write down your feelings. What emotions do these memories evoke?

_____

_____

_____

_____

3. Can you see yourself forgiving that person? Can you see yourself loving that person? Hopefully, by the end of this book, the answer to this question will be yes if it is no right now.

_____

Let's go to the Lord in prayer:

Father God, You are so powerful and wonderful. Our eyes have not seen nor our ears have heard the wonders of Your mighty love for us. Father, the names and circumstances that we have written down represent the people who have hurt us deeply, beyond comprehension, and beyond any pain we have ever felt or known before. You know our hearts and how, at times, we hate these people and relish the thought of getting even with them for hurting us. This is not Your way, Father. We offer these people and the circumstances for our hurt to you right now. Please take our hurt and pain and show us how to forgive and how to see them as you see them. Please help us, Father, to heal, take away our guilt, pain, shame, and unforgiveness. Teach us to trust You and let go. We ask this in the precious name of our Lord and Savior, Jesus Christ. Amen.

Sins of Omission and Generational Sin Equals Abuse

> Her brother Absalom said to her, "Has that Ammon, your brother, been with you? Be quiet now, my sister, he is your brother. Don't take this thing to heart." And Tamar lived in her brother Absalom's house, a desolate woman. When King David heard all this, he was furious.
>
> 2 Samuel 13:20–21

It is amazing to me how history repeats itself over and over again. King David, while he was furious and burned with anger at the reality of his daughter being raped by her brother Ammon, did nothing. He allowed Ammon to get away with this abuse without confrontation or one word of rebuke! My father is very much like King David in this instance, because he turned a blind eye to the abuse of his children.

Like my counselor said, "Come on! Your father knew and chose not to make waves or confront your mother." She was right. This was the hardest truth for me to accept and deal with. I had put my father on a pedestal. He could do no wrong in my eyes. He was my hero, and I was truly Daddy's little girl. It was easier to forgive my father than it was to forgive my mother, but it was harder for me to accept the truth of his omission to protect us.

Ephesians 6:4 says, "Fathers, do not exasperate your children; instead, bring them up in the training and instruction of the Lord." Notice that this scripture does not reference mothers bringing up or training the children? This is the exclusive right of the father. Now, you single moms out there have to do what you have to do, and I am sorry that your mate is not available to help rear your children. I am talking mainly to married couples—one man and one woman—who are raising children together. To my father's credit, he never raised an ugly hand to his children. He never hit us or beat us. However, when my dad raised his voice and we knew he was angry, we snapped to attention and did whatever he asked. My father had our respect whereas my mother didn't.

The worst thing you can do if you know someone is being abused is to remain silent. By your silence, you are saying that the abuse committed is okay in your eyes. This is the sin of omission.

I remember one time when my father could have spoke up and told the truth about what he knew; instead he chose to turn a blind eye and pretend that the abuse was not real. The story goes like this:

My brother and I had just gotten new bikes for our birthdays. I was eight, and my brother was six. My brother was quite the daredevil, and he knew no fear when it came to riding bikes, jumping with bikes, or racing down hills at incredible speeds. It was a thrill for him. It was a beautiful, sunny day, and my brother and I were at the top of a hill in our neighborhood with our bikes. My brother got the brilliant idea of riding our bikes down the hill at the same time. My little brother had the best ideas! Off we went down the hill together on our bikes. Uh oh! Look out! A turn! One bike went slamming into the other and down we went. My brother got the worst of the pavement, and when we finally got home, my dad had to take him to the hospital. I was scraped up pretty good but didn't need stitches of any kind.

I remember when they got home from the hospital. My dad had ice cream! Ice cream always made the hurts feel better. At dinner, my mother and father were talking about the bike accident, and I can remember my father saying something like, "Funny thing the doctor asked today. He asked if our son was being beaten or abused." What I didn't realize is that my brother had to take off his clothes to be examined by the doctor. The doctor saw the stripes on his back, legs, and buttocks. My dad denied the truth right there and covered up the sins of my mother.

How this brings scores of tears to my eyes today. The one chance that a stranger could have stepped in and helped and did nothing. When memories like this come back, an automatic prayer goes up: "Father, forgive me, for at this moment it is very difficult for me not to hate my mother. Give me Your love to love her and the ability to forgive her yet again. In Jesus's name, amen." Sometimes I say this prayer over and over until I feel God taking the hate away again, and His mercy, grace, and love come flowing into my Spirit.

I am sure there were other instances when strangers suspected the abuse, but no one came forward and no one helped, and the abuse continued. If you know someone who is being abused, I beg you, please, do not turn a blind eye. Get involved! Please! How I wish someone had gotten involved all those years ago. If you don't want to get involved, then call Protective Services in your community. In our community, you can call Protective Services and remain anonymous. Please don't allow the abuse to continue, you may just save a life.

Generational Sin

> You shall not bow down to them or worship them; for I, the LORD your God, am a jealous God, punishing the children for the sin of the fathers to the third and fourth generation of those who hate me, but showing love to a thousand generations to those who love me and keep my commandments.
>
> Exodus 20:5–6

Sins of the fathers—this does not just apply to idol worshiping but in disobeying God. Disobeying God can also mean abusing the gifts He has given to you, i.e., children.

Generational sin is very real, and you can take God's Word for the absolute truth. I will walk you through the generational sin that led to my mother's abuse of my brother and me, the abuse both my parents suffered at the hands of their fathers, and the potential for continued abuse had I had children. Thankfully, there is help, and you can stop the cycle of sin that leads to abuse if you seek God and get the necessary help you need.

I will start with my mother. After the memories started to unblock, I had to find answers to why this happened. After all, it had not always been like this. My mother was kind and loving when we lived near Detroit and didn't raise an ugly voice or hand to us until we moved north. So what happened? I went to my other grandmother, my mother's mother, and started asking questions. I just knew there had to be an explanation or answer for my mother's abusive actions. What I learned was astonishing. What God says about punishing the sins of the father to the third and fourth generation was ringing true in this family! Check out this chain of abuse:

1. My great-grandfather (my mother's grandfather) had been abused by his father! I don't have the details of what was done, but from the events leading up to my abuse, it was pretty severe.

2. My grandfather (my mother's father) had been abused by his father (great-grandfather referenced above). Are you following me here? We already have generational sin going on. Great-Grandpa was abused by his father, and my grandfather was abused by his father. See the pattern? My grandfather had a disease called colitis. This is a disease wherein you can't always control your bowels and you could have an accident in your pants if you couldn't get to a bathroom in time. Well, my grandfather's father did not understand this disease and accused my grandfather of being lazy and unclean, as opposed to having a disease or illness and having an accident. My grandfather was beaten severely with

belts, attacked with a pitchfork, and beaten with fists and boards of wood. They lived on and owned a farm, and Great-Grandpa would frequently abuse the farm animals by jabbing a pitchfork into them. My great-grandfather also sexually molested my mother. She was not raped, but she was touched in unhealthy ways.

3. My mother and her brother were abused by my grandfather (their father). My grandfather would frequently beat his children with belts and his fists. One memory my grandmother shared with me was a time when my uncle was very young, maybe ten, and he had eaten several chocolate chip cookies before breakfast. Well, my grandfather was really angry with my uncle and was going to teach him a lesson. So he cooked up a mess of pancakes and forced my uncle to eat all of them! My uncle's stomach could have ruptured, and he could have died. As it was, I believe my uncle suffered a terrible stomachache and may have ended up throwing up. When my grandmother shared this reality with me, I sobbed and sobbed at the reality I was looking at. The sins of the father will reach the third and fourth generation.

4. My brother and I are the fourth generation to be abused, and you have read our story in the first chapter of this book. The only difference is that we were abused by our mother and not our father.

Do you see the pattern here? I remember my grandmother telling me that my grandfather rationalized his abuse of his children by saying, "If it was good enough for me, then it is good enough for my children." Thankfully, my grandmother had the sense to step in and threatened divorce if he continued to abuse the children as well as her.

My grandfather beat my grandmother as well. He slapped her around and beat her with his fists. By the time my grandmother finally put a stop to all the abuse, the example was ingrained in my mother's head, and it was far too late. She needed counseling immediately to deal with the scars and pain of her own abuse, but she did not get the help she needed. To this day, she has not dealt with that pain or acknowledged the effects that it has had on her life.

━━━━━━━━━━

Now let's take a look at my father's history of abuse. Unfortunately, I don't know much about my father's history. This side of the family didn't talk much about past history. What I have learned is that my father's father was abusive and an alcoholic. He would drink his paychecks away at the local bar and then come home and knock his wife and three sons around. My father has refused to answer my questions about the details of his childhood and those of my uncles, but from talking to cousins, I have gleaned that it was not always a pleasant home to be in.

I remembered when my grandfather died. I can remember my father saying something like, "Good riddance." This obviously leaves a lot of unanswered questions. My father's parents were from a different country and didn't speak much English. Toward the end of my grandfather's life, he had selective hearing. You know what that is, don't you? It is when an elderly person is going deaf or is hard of hearing but conveniently pretends not to hear questions posed to him by a certain inquisitive granddaughter. Tight-lipped and sealed mouth was my answer.

━━━━━━━━━━

The effects of abuse severely affected my brother, and today he is hot-tempered and quick to anger. He has been in countless fights and has quite the police record. To a certain degree, he has carried on the abuse he received as a child to other people instead of children. My brother is not married and has had one if not two children out of wedlock. Both children have been adopted out. Because of his experiences at church and the phoniness of the messages, he is a self-proclaimed atheist. I pray for him every day and ask God to open his blind eyes and unlock his deaf ears. There is a God, and He loves us and you very much. It was never God's intention that you or I or my brother or anyone suffer or be subjected to abuse. Please hear me on this. God loves you! It is not that God wants us to suffer; He allows people to make their own choices—good or evil. It is called freewill.

> For though we walk in the flesh, we do not war after the flesh; for the weapons of our warfare are not carnal, but mighty through God to the pulling down of strongholds casting down imaginations, and every high thing that exalts itself against the knowledge of God, and bringing into captivity every thought to the obedience of Christ.
>
> 2 Corinthians 10:3–5

Did you catch that? We don't war against the flesh. We war against the evil one of this world. We are creatures who have a sin nature in us, and we can easily be tempted or led astray, just as easily as Eve was tempted and led astray in the garden of Eden. Every one of my grandfathers had the ability to stop the generational sin and step out in faith, but they didn't. More children were abused, more pain was inflicted; and more anger and rage were not dealt with properly.

I would ask you to take a look at your own life at this point. Do you know your family history? Who in your family has been abused and who was the abuser? Make a list and chart your family history. If it is a boyfriend or husband who was the abuser, do the same with his family history. Chances are that if you look closely, you will see generational sin. Remember to always hate the sin and not the person. Forgive the person who has hurt you and pray for him or her.

If you are currently in an abusive situation—leave! Get out now! Go to a friend's home, your church, or your local police department. God does not expect you to stay with people who are abusing you, even if it means no contact with your own family. I will explain more about that in a later chapter.

===

Now, let's take a look at how I was allowing generational sin to repeat itself yet again. Would I stop it or would I continue the cycle? I thank God almost every day that my husband and I were not blessed with children.

Matthew and I had been married for two years and decided we wanted to get a dog. We had two cats that we adored but felt that we wanted a dog for protection as well, as we felt this would complete our little family since we had decided not to have children. Every home needs a dog, right? God blessed us with a beautiful Norwegian Elk Hound.

It wasn't long after our new friend started living with us that my generational sin tendencies started taking over. I was angry and full of rage and hate, but I didn't understand or realize why. Most of the memories were still blocked, and I had not dealt with my hate, anger, or pain at that point. Our new friend started barking a lot and was not really house trained. I started repeating the sin of my mother.

One day, I was yelling at the dog and all of a sudden I looked deeply into his big brown eyes. I stopped immediately as a voice came into my mind and said, "Why do you hate me? Why do you hurt me? Why are you so angry and hateful toward me? I was given to you to bring you pleasure and protection. I was given to you so you could run your fingers through my soft fur and be comforted when you simply needed something to hold on to." I sank to the floor sobbing and crying into his fur, telling this beautiful dog I was sorry for hurting him. I petted him and held him for a long time, and when I got up I don't know who was more covered in tears, me or his fur.

Was it my dog's voice I heard? Well, I won't know for sure until I get to heaven and ask God, but I believe God allowed my dog to speak to my heart. I believe God allowed my dog to communicate with me in that moment in an attempt to get me to see my sin against His creation as well as to help me see the cycle of sin. Oh, so you don't believe that you can communicate with animals? Let's take a look at Scripture to see if the animals really could communicate with us.

In the beginning, Adam and Eve were able to communicate with the animals. They could talk and understand them, and the animals could talk and understand the humans. Don't believe me? Check out this passage of Scripture:

> Now the LORD God had formed out of the ground all the beasts of the field and all the birds of the air. He brought them to the man to see what he would name them; and whatever the man called each living creature, that was its name. So the man gave names to all the beasts of the field… Now the serpent was more crafty than any of the wild animals the LORD God had made. He *said* to the woman, "Did God really say You must not eat from any tree in the garden?" (Emphasis mine)
>
> Genesis 2:19–20, 3:1

Did you catch that? The serpent *said* to the woman—the serpent spoke to Eve! Now, if a snake started speaking to me in my language, I would have been afraid, maybe started yelling, and would have been totally amazed that this creature could talk to me and even more amazed that we could understand each other. Was Eve amazed? Was she baffled that this snake could talk to her? No! She didn't think twice about the snake talking to her. Why? Because the animals that God created could communicate with Adam and Eve, and they could communicate with the animals. Otherwise, don't you think she would have cried out to the Father and told Him that something very weird was happening—a snake spoke to her! Eve did not do this; in fact, she carried on the conversation with the serpent or snake just as she probably carried on conversations with other critters God had created and allowed to wonder in His garden.

After the fall of man, that all changed and we could no longer understand the animals. God saw fit to take that blessing away. In Genesis 3:14, we read: "So the Lord God said to the serpent, 'Because you have done this, cursed are you above all the livestock and all the wild animals! You will crawl on your belly and you will eat dust all the days of your life.'"

God cursed the animals as well as humans for our disobedience. No longer could we commune with the animals or them with us.

I believe that my dog was allowed to communicate with me. In that moment, I realized that I had become my mother! This simply had to stop. I felt God calling me to end generational sin. The question was how.

The first step in ending this generational sin was to take control of my life and no longer allow my mother to influence my decisions or life in negative ways. You see, the physical abuse stopped when I was fourteen, but the emotional abuse continued in the form of attempted control over the life of my husband and me and our decisions.

We were renting my grandmother's home that my father had inherited at the time of my grandparents' death. At first, I was ecstatic! I was living in the very home that was my place of refuge when I was a child. I could remember my grandmother clearly protecting me, and I felt her presence very strongly. We lived in this place for two years.

My husband and I were still newly married. We got married in September, and I discovered I was pregnant in December. Then I lost the baby through a miscarriage in February. Even though we did not want children, I was still devastated and blamed myself. I called my mother (who had suffered a tubular pregnancy and lost two babies through miscarriage), thinking she would at least understand what I was going through. Instead of giving me the support, love, and understanding I desperately needed, she asked me, "How do you know you were pregnant?"

There was no sympathy, no empathy, and no love. I called my favorite aunt and told her what had happened. She provided the love and support that should have come from my mother. After I lost the baby, I was not properly taken care of and ended up getting a bacterial and yeast infection due to not being thoroughly cleaned out after miscarrying. This devastated me even more, and I slipped into depression. This incident was the one that propelled me to get out from under the control of my mother once and for all. It was time to move!

One day, I started packing. My husband and I decided that we wanted to purchase our own home and truly be out from under the control of my mother. My husband didn't understand why I was packing when we didn't even know where we were moving and didn't have a home secured. I felt that I was being led by God and just knew that we had to be ready. Six months later, we moved into our new home.

Moving did not decrease the control my mother had; it only intensified it. My mother would drop over unannounced, tell me how to arrange or rearrange my home and the furnishings, how to set up my kitchen, and where this or that should go. In once sense, I felt I was still a little girl living under my mother's roof.

Ephesians 6:31 says, "For this reason a man will leave his father and mother and be united to his wife, and the two will become one flesh." My parents had been allowed to become totally independent from their parents; why weren't we being allowed this same respect? In a word—control. My mother is very controlling and has to be in control of every aspect of my life, or so she believes. I realized that by allowing my mother to control our lives as husband and wife, I was disobeying God and what He calls us to be—one man and one woman united before God and living under His control alone.

After the miscarriage of our baby and the realization of my tendency to continue the generational sin, my husband and I decided we definitely did not want to have children. We knew we didn't want children before, but were willing to raise a child if an "accident" happened. After this incident, we started taking precautionary measures to ensure that I would not get pregnant.

This is a very sensitive subject, and it was not a decision we made haphazardly. At this point, we had not put our faith and trust in Jesus Christ, but we, nonetheless, felt God pulling us in a different direction and later would realize that we had sought the will of God for our lives. He was working on us even before we knew or wanted to know him! I thank God every day that He closed my womb and has left me barren. I was determined that the generational sin would end with me, even if that meant sacrificing the blessing of having children.

After making this decision permanent, my mother started pressuring us to have children. We explained to her that first, it was none of her business; this was a very personal decision between a husband and wife and second, we had made the decision final and we would not be having children.

Also, the fact remained that my mother abused my brother and me; would she do the same to my children, her grandchildren? I had no reason to think she had changed. Knowing the laws for grandparental rights, a fear shot through me like an arrow that I would have to allow my mother access to my children. No way! What guarantee did I have that she would not abuse my children when they upset her? None. Case closed: we were not having children. It was a sacrifice, but it was for the best, and God has and will continue to reward us for sacrificing the joy of becoming parents.

Generational sin is very real and does exist. If our decision not to have children has saved the life of a child from continued generational sin and abuse, then the sacrifice was well worth the pain and emptiness of not having children.

As I close this chapter, let's review the facts:

1. Sins of omission are just as great as sins of abuse. When my father chose to look the other way, he sinned. My brother and I were placed in his care for protection, love, and safety. He let us down by looking the other way and refusing to confront or get involved in the abuse issue.

2. Generational sin is real and does exist. I am the fourth generation of abused children, and I know in my heart of hearts that had I had children, I would have continued the cycle of abuse. I would never lay an ugly hand

on a child that was not mine, but I could not make the same guarantee about my own children because of my past experiences. I had the abuse seed in me, and I had my mother's genes.

3. Sometimes it takes sacrifice to end generational sin. Our decision not to have children was difficult, but necessary to ensure that the generational sin would not be repeated. It had to stop.

4. People who have been abused tend to want to control every aspect of their lives as well as other people's lives because they themselves had no control when they were abused. I was headed in that direction. It wasn't until I totally surrendered to God and laid down my hate, anger, and rage that I was truly able to forgive my mother and release the curse of generational sin that had afflicted this family for too many generations. Soon I would be free at last to live in Christ!

Questions to Ponder

1. Take a look, again, at your family tree. Do you know of people in your immediate history that have been abused? Has that abuse carried on?

---

2. How about you? Have you carried generational sin into your life? Do you find yourself abusing the children God gifted to you? How about your spouse? Do you nag? Do you yell or scream? How about your language? Do you use ugly words to get a point across? How do you feel toward certain people or certain groups of people? Are you holding innocent people hostage because someone in one of those groups abused you?

---

3. Do you know someone who is being abused? Have you looked the other way or would you dare to step out in faith, get involved, and save a life? When you can put your pride down and when you truly don't care what other people think of you, then you can be used by God to do amazing things, even things like save the life of someone who is being abused.

_____

_____

_____

_____

Let's go to the Father in prayer:

Father God, thank you for loving us, your children! Father, children are gifts to all kinds of peoples of this world. I would pray right now if someone has generational sin in his or her life, please open his or her eyes to Your truth. Please grant us the courage and strength to come forward with boldness to speak up and be your hands and feet to the abused, lost, and hurting of this world. I ask it in Jesus's name. Amen.

Forgiveness
Equals Healing

If my people, who are called by my name, will humble themselves
and pray and seek my face and turn from their wicked ways,
then will I hear from heaven and will forgive their sin and will
heal their land.

2 Chronicles 7:14

After doing the research and finding out about generational sin, I
discovered that I had a lot of rage, anger, hate, and unforgiveness
within me, but God was calling me to a better life. Did you know
that it can feel good, for a time, to hang on to the ugly emotions
such as hate, anger, and unforgiveness? For a time, I actually enjoyed
hating my mother and blaming her for everything that went wrong
in my life.

It felt good to point a finger at the one who was to blame for my
anger, hate, and all my problems. It was *her!* She did this! She did
it to me! It's all her fault my business failed; it's all her fault I am
fighting with my husband; it is all her fault that I don't have the life
I have always dreamed of having! Right?

Don't buy into this lie from the evil one. When you become old
enough to discern right from wrong, you no longer have an excuse for
the willful sin in your life. It is a choice. You can choose to do the right
thing or you can choose to continue sinning, but the choice is yours.

There was an ugly beast deep within my being that ached to get
out and wanted to destroy and hurt the person that hurt me so badly.

That beast and those feelings are not of God, and it had to go. By allowing the negative emotions and feelings to build up, not releasing them, but pushing them further into my being, my body was screaming for help. The only way my body could get my attention was to break down.

God has a way of leading us down different paths in an attempt to get us to look up and acknowledge Him. I was full of sin and I was starting to feel the stirrings and longings to get back to a church. My husband would have none of it. He thought church was boring and had no interest in worshiping a God he could not see. Well, that made sense to me, and so we stayed away from church for a while. Thankfully, God doesn't give up, and He allowed me to travel deeper into my sin and destructive ways before rescuing me from the miry pit. The hate, anger, and rage I had felt toward my mother were starting to surface

We then moved to a little village and God started calling my heart. I found a little church and started attending by myself. My husband refused to go and did not have an interest in church at all. I never pressured him, because I knew that would only drive him away. So I went to church and didn't say much, but started getting filled up and felt the calling of God on my heart.

One Sunday, I came home and my husband asked me how it was. This was different. I started telling him about this incredible band that played and—wait, incredible band? What band? "You never said anything about a band before! There is a band at church; with drums and electric guitars?" Well, that got his attention. My husband and I are very much into music, and music is a large part of our life, even to this day. I told him about the band and how wonderful and "rock us" the music was. The next Sunday passed and I went alone, but then came a time when my husband started attending with me. That was the start of our faith together.

At this point in my life my husband and I were living in our own home; we had just started attending church as a couple; we were making a go of it in the workforce; the miscarriage debacle was over and we were moving forward with our lives. We had our two cats and our dog.

You have heard that when someone has been abused, he or she will sometimes seek out people who will carry on the abuse, i.e., an abused spouse. Well, in my case, I didn't choose an abusive spouse, but I did choose abusive employers. Not intentionally, mind you, but I believe subconsciously I went and worked for the familiar and found myself working for abusive bosses who created a lot of tension and stress for me.

I had worked in a few very stressful jobs where my employers were less than kind. This just compounded the hate and anger I had already felt. It also kept fueling my justifications for hating people. Under all of this stress and negativity, my body began to break down, and I developed a skin disorder caused by Candida. Candida is an overgrowth of yeast in the body and can manifest itself into many different symptoms, mocking many different diseases. The beast was trying to get out! I was covered from head to toe with hives. These are huge ugly welts that itch and burn and hurt and ooze nasty serum and blood.

I was not dealing with my anger and the ugly emotions that I needed to deal with. I would push them down and attempt to ignore them. I went to a few doctors and they could not help me. They put me on a bunch of medication that literally almost put me in the grave. There is a whole other book on this subject, so I won't go into all of the horrific details now. I will say that God placed a very loving, caring, and special person in my life that led me to the cure of my hives. We took an organic, supplemental path, and within one week my hives were gone for good and I was on the road to healing physically. That, however, did not heal my broken spirit or heart.

After I healed physically, I wanted to share these newfound products with the people that I loved. I knew that if these products helped me, then they could help other people as well. I started a business selling these products and invited my family over for a meeting to introduce them to these products and my new friends in the business.

It turned out that my parents had dabbled in this same business when I was a child, but it did not prove lucrative for them and they got out. At this business meeting in our home, all my parents did was play devil's advocate and put down the products or attempt to put down my new friends at every turn. I was mortified at their behavior and clearly saw their immaturity.

My dad claimed the products were snake oil and my mother proceeded to tell my new friend that she was acting irresponsible when she gave a child who had a headache a B vitamin supplement. I couldn't understand their negativity since the products had worked so well for me and had helped other people to heal from all sorts of physical ailments.

My husband and I dove head and feet first into the business because we had a strong desire to help other people, not to get rich. We worked this business for ten years and ended up walking away from it because we simply were not reaching the people as we had hoped. However, before we gave up our business, I joined a group of business entrepreneurs in an attempt to get this business off the ground. It was in this business group of professionals I met my counselor. Yes, God works in mysterious ways!

My counselor, Joanna, and I hit it off immediately. I just loved this woman and felt she could help the inner beast that lived inside me to finally go away. At the same time, I had been invited by some women in our church to join a Bible study class on forgiveness.

During this counseling period, I was also attending a Bible study group on forgiveness. Matthew and I had been attending church for a couple of years by now, still not saved but learning a lot, and there was a notice in the church bulletin that offered a Bible study course for women only for people who had been abused and how to deal with that anger. I told Matthew I felt this Bible study was for me. During the Bible study, it was strongly suggested that we also attend counseling sessions. I had already started seeing Joanna when I joined this group, so I was covered there.

Let me back up a bit here so you can get a better understanding of what had transformed between losing my grandmother and the decision to start going to church. I had felt that something was missing in our lives. Matthew and I had lived in our home we had purchased for about five years, and one day I started to attend the local church in our village alone. At this point, we had not accepted Jesus as our Lord and Savior, but we believed in God. I had been raised in a church, and my husband had been taken to church by his mother and grandparents on Christmas and Easter holidays with no real understanding or meaning. We both knew there was a God, but we didn't know Him or His Son until much later.

Was meeting my counselor at this business group meeting a coincidence? I think not!

I started meeting with Joanna once or twice per week, sorting out my thoughts, feelings and attempting to understand why a mother would abuse her own child. I had way too much anger in me, and I was afraid of allowing this anger beast to come out for fear that I could really hurt someone with my words or worse. I had never taken a look at the damage the abuse had caused. Not just the physical damage, but the mental, emotional, and spiritual damage that had broken my heart.

Joanna gave me permission to yell, scream, pound pillows and couches, and shake the trees as hard as I could. It was so very difficult for me to do this. I just couldn't let go like that. I even dared to scream at God, "Why? Why God? Why would you allow a little child to suffer so much pain? Why was I born? Why did you place me with this family? Why did I have to suffer so much?" I was starting to feel like Job.

Have you ever done this? It is a weird feeling to let the anger out if you are not used to letting go like that.

Beth Moore was our teacher through her wonderful video series called *Breaking Free*. I owe a lot to Beth. If I ever get the chance, I would love to thank her in person for allowing God to work through her, because through her material in *Breaking Free*, God was finally able to touch my heart and break through the solid rock of cement I had built up around my heart.

It turns out that Beth and I have quite a bit in common. She was abused too, but not in the same way I was. Remember, abuse is abuse is abuse, and no matter what type of abuse you have suffered, it does the same thing to your heart, spirit, and soul. Beth explained the pain she had suffered. She had lived and dealt with the same anger, rage, and hatred I had experienced. She had acted out in similar ways like I had, i.e., poor relationships. For the first time in my life, I realized that I was not alone in the abuse I suffered. Someone else in this world understood and went through the same feelings, emotions, and difficulties in relationships I had gone through. Someone else had experienced the same pain and suffering I had. I felt like there may be hope for me yet, that maybe I could be healed; I could be whole; I could stop being so afraid.

As I moved through the Bible study and got deeper into Beth's series on forgiveness, God kept the pressure on. I shared with my Bible study group about my abuse and the effects it had on my life. Do you know what they had the nerve to say to me? They told me I needed to forgive! Can you believe that? Forgive? My mother? The person who wounded my heart and spirit and soul? After all, I was justified in hating her.

The world told me that I had every right to be angry; I had every right to hang on to that anger as long as I wanted; I had every right to do whatever I wanted. I called this wrestling with God. Remember when Jacob wrestled with God?

> Then the man said, "Your name will no longer be Jacob, but Israel, because you have struggled with God and with men and have overcome."
>
> Genesis 32:28

I wrestled with God. I didn't want to forgive my mother. I wanted her to suffer as much as she had made me suffer. Refusing to forgive someone is like drinking rat poison and expecting the other person to die. The only person you are hurting by not forgiving is you, not the person who abused you.

═══════════════
═══════════════

I was beginning to see the light. I finally understood the abuse cycle, generational sin, and the sin of control and pride. God was calling me to forgive my mother and move forward, but I was trying to tune Him out and really didn't want to forgive my mother. I wanted to hate her.

After all, she was the reason my life was so messed up, right? Wrong! My life was messed up because I refused to forgive someone who had deeply wounded me. The pressure was on! God was not going to give up until I forgave the one who had hurt me so deeply, and I was not going to forgive because I was justified and had a good reason to hang on to that hate.

I can remember the day as clearly as if it were yesterday. It was a crisp November day just before Thanksgiving. Our Bible study group had almost finished the course, and I was meeting with my counselor once a week. I was on my lunch hour and was listening to the radio and a sermon series by Nancy Leigh DeMoss. What was her topic? Yes, you guessed it: forgiveness. Nancy was talking about forgiving those who had wounded us deeply and said that God could not, nor would He, bless us unless we forgave those who deeply hurt us. She then said that God knew our hurts, our wounds, and that He would bring justice and make things right, but it was His timing and His way and not ours. I got up and shut my office door.

The tears came and I went back and read Beth's chapter on forgiveness. Beth and Nancy's words intermingled and they both said the same thing: forgive. Give all your hurt, pain, anger, rage, and hate to God. He can handle it. He will deal with it. He will put things right and will heal your broken heart. God won and I bowed my head, and with tears streaming down my face, with the memories flooding back, and the emotions of the pain, helplessness, shame, hurt, anger, and rage coursing through my body, heart, mind, and spirit, I released and gave it all up to God. I prayed and told God He could have all of it—all the hurt and negative feelings. I released my mother into His hands and truly, from my heart, forgave her. I told God I did not want to take revenge on her, that His justice and mercy would be sufficient. Finally, at the end of that prayer, I asked Jesus to come into my life—truly and honestly accepting Him for the very first time in my life to be my personal Lord and Savior, asked Him to forgive my sins and to guide my life from that day forward. I closed my prayer with a heartfelt thank you and amen.

Freedom at last! It felt like a ton of bricks had literally fallen from my shoulders. I felt free! I felt cleansed from the inside out. I felt the stirrings of life deep within my spirit. I felt God. This freedom can be yours too. God is no respecter of persons, and He loves all of us because He created us; we are His children.

I have a hard time describing what happened next. It was nothing less than a miracle. I felt washed, cleansed, and happy. Tears of joy had replaced the tears of bitterness, pain, and shame. I literally could not find one ounce of anger, hate, rage, or other negative feeling inside me. I looked deep and even brought back a painful memory, but nothing. No bad feelings. It was all gone, completely and totally gone! I had been scrubbed clean on the inside, and I praised God and laughingly asked Him why He hadn't allowed me to do this sooner. I could almost see Him looking down at me saying, "Child, I have been after you to forgive your mother for months now. Why didn't *you* decide to forgive earlier?" I felt so drained but at the same time so full of joy.

━━━━━━━━━━

Before I go further, if you have not accepted Jesus as your personal Lord and Savior and asked Him to come into your life, I would strongly encourage you to do that right now. He loves you. Speaking from experience here, it was a *huge* leap of faith for me to trust in Him and simply let go. If I can do it, I know you can. It wasn't easy for me to make that decision but once I did, I was not disappointed. I struggle with receiving love even to this day, but I know without a doubt that my Lord loves me and cares for me, and He loves you too.

━━━━━━━━━━

For me, that day was the start of a continuing and ongoing stream of forgiveness. Just because you forgive one time doesn't mean you are done forgiving. This is a process that continues over a lifetime. There are still memories that come back that I have to lift to God and hand to Him in total surrender and forgiveness. There are times when I want to hate my mother for what she did to my brother and me, but I have to hand that over as well.

I thank God that He is bigger than all of my hate, anger, wounds, and pain. He just keeps on taking all I have to give Him and He is constantly replacing those negative feelings with joy and peace. By the way, you can't ever fool God. Sometimes, I say I have forgiven and I can almost see God saying, "Are you sure? Have you really?"

"Yes, of course," is my reply. That is your cue to reexamine your heart and see if you are holding any negative feelings or emotions toward the person who hurt you. Remember, this is an ongoing process. The initial forgiving that I did was real and did come from the heart; however, as newer memories come to the surface, I have to forgive those as well.

> Then Peter came to Jesus and asked, "LORD, how many times shall I forgive my brother when he sins against me? Up to seven times?" Jesus answered, "I tell you, not seven times, but seventy-seven times."
>
> Matthew 18:21–22

You can't just forgive one time and be done with it. You have to forgive every time you are tempted to hate the person who hurt or wounded you. If you are not sincere in your forgiveness, then God will place someone in your path that will test what you claim. This happened to me.

You must truly forgive from your heart, mind, and spirit. You can't fool God, for He knows you better than you know yourself. It is okay to be angry, but don't sin in that anger. I think that when we sin in our anger, it allows the old us to come out and we recognize that we still have some forgiving to do. Let me give you an example of how God tested my forgiveness toward my mother.

I was working in a judicial system, and I was responsible for working with people who had committed crimes against society. A few days after I had forgiven my mother, I was tested in my claim. God placed a woman in my office who was convicted of abusing her children and was threatened with having them taken away. Well, that got my ire up! As I was looking over her case, I felt my heart go cold, and I was thinking to myself that I would set this woman up for failure. I would set the bar too high, knowing she would not be able to comply. I would make sure she'd pay for what she did to her children.

Then I heard it. It wasn't an audible sound, but it was a definite thought: *Child! What are you doing? You are to treat all people who come to your office the same—no favorites, no differential treatment for anyone. Who made you judge, jury, and executioner of this woman? When did I give you authority to emit justice? Didn't you say that you had forgiven and didn't you hand your thoughts of getting even to Me?* Uh oh! I knew that voice! I had heard it before, but it was softer before. I knew this was God, and I knew if I went ahead with my plan to hurt this woman and carry out the punishment even more than what she was facing, I would be in big trouble with my Savior, Jesus, and His Father, my Father, God.

I quickly made the wrong right and showed compassion on this woman. Ironically, when she left my office, she thanked me for being so kind and blessed me! Wow! The point is if you forgive someone for something, rest assured God will test your honesty in truly forgiving that person.

Something else that happened and was truly a miracle is that when I forgave and truly handed the Lord my heart, He placed a new heart in me. Prior to totally releasing all of the ugly emotions and non-forgiveness to God, I had harbored absolute hatred toward people in my heart. It scares me to think what I would have done or would have been capable of doing had God not gotten a hold of me when He did. Praise the Lord for His redemptive power!

I hated people with a passion. I didn't want to be around them, didn't want to socialize with them much, and certainly didn't want any new friends in my life. I was married and I loved my husband (and still do!), but he reminded me of my grandmother and had the same kindly traits that she had. I didn't have many friends and certainly no real close friends that I could confide in. I didn't go out with the girls, nor did I enjoy shopping or being out in public. In hindsight, all this hate was really not trusting in people and self-protection. To this day, I still don't like shopping, but I have a few very close Christian girlfriends that I am able to confide in and trust. I still struggle with trust issues, but God continues to work on me in that area.

When I gave my heart to Christ and forgave those who hurt me, I started to look at people differently. I actually had compassion on people, especially those who were lost (didn't know Christ) and suffering. I would weep as they told me their life story, and I found myself amazed at the abundance of compassion and love I felt toward them. I am telling you, this was a true miracle, because this was not me! I hated people! If you know your Bible, then you might remember the story of Paul, formerly Saul.

Saul hated Christians, hated them with a passion, until Jesus got a hold of him on the road to Damascus, showed His glory all around Paul, blinded him for three days, and set the truth in his heart. After that, Paul gave his life to Christ and became a devote follower, considering himself the "least of these" as a disciple. Read Acts 11 in your Bible for the whole story of Paul.

To give you an idea of how much hate and anger had festered in my heart, I will use Paul as an example again and the scripture in Acts 7:59–60. I will paraphrase the story. Saul (who became Paul on the road to Damascus) watched and gave approval of the stoning death of Stephen, a disciple and follower of Christ Jesus. He watched Stephen get stoned to death and actually enjoyed the show! You can almost hear the snickering from Saul when they were stoning Stephen. Saul gave his approval and watched as other people stoned Stephen to death! Can you feel the hatred Saul had for Stephen? I sure can. In fact, the hatred Saul had for Stephen is the same hatred I had for all people! Not just Christians or any set group of people, but for all human beings! This was a direct psychological result of being abused. And, like Paul, it wasn't until the Lord Jesus Christ got a hold of me and opened my eyes to His truth that my heart started to change. All people are created in the image of God. So to hate people was ultimately hating God. Yikes!

Please let me reassure you here. If you have been abused to the point that you do hate people, take heart. I know how you feel; I have been there. I know the pain; I know the anger; I know that it is easier to hate than to love when you yourself have been so wounded. I know that very well, and you have my compassion and love for you and your situation. However, if you allow God to get a hold of your heart, He will show you and bring people into your life that you can trust and that you can love. He will give you a new heart. Second Corinthians 5:17 says, "Therefore, if anyone is in Christ, he is a new creation; the old has gone, the new has come!" That is so true! All of that hate and anger I held toward all people was gone the instant that I accepted Jesus Christ as my Lord and Savior and forgave the person who did the unthinkable damage to me. All of that hate and anger was gone in an instant! I literally felt it leaving my heart, mind, and body. I started seeing people in a different light and actually felt and had compassion on them! What a change!

Let's review the facts:

1. Grouping the type of person who abused you into a hate category with all people is wrong. That is sin. Another example of this: A woman is raped and afterward she blames or develops a hatred for all men. That is sin. Not all men raped her. So to hate all men is wrong. When we have been wounded to the very core of our being, it is very difficult not to hate. That is why

we must forgive those who hurt us so deeply and turn the negative emotions over to God.

2. If you keep your hatred, anger, rage, pain, and other negative emotions and feelings bottled up inside you without any type of release, it will cause your body to break down. The evil will find a way out somehow, whether that shows up in physical ailments, mental or emotional issues, or spiritual meltdown.

3. You must face your abuse. You must peel back the layers of hurt and pain and look at it for what it is. You cannot blame yourself for what another has done to you. It was not your fault. You didn't ask to be abused, and you did absolutely nothing to deserve the treatment you received by your abusers.

4. Jesus Christ is the only One who can forgive you of your sins and save your life from eternal damnation. He is the truth, the way, and the life, and no one comes to the Almighty Father unless he accepts Jesus, His Son, as his personal Savior. There is no back way into heaven. Jesus is the bridge, and if you don't take that bridge, you will not go to heaven.

Questions to Ponder

1. Do you have negative feelings toward someone who hurt you? Have you pushed these feelings down so far that it may be affecting your heath?

2. Do you group people into a category to justify your hate and anger? An example of this would be to hate all men because a man raped you or to hate all women because a woman abused you. How about this one: hate all people of a certain color because of abuse that happened generations ago? Uh oh, I think I struck a nerve somewhere. I love all people today because Christ got a hold of my heart. Just because your ancestors were slaves does not mean you can hate the people of today for that horrific abuse of yesterday. Let it go!

_____

_____

_____

_____

3. Have you received counseling for the abuse you have suffered? I would strongly recommend finding a Christian counselor in your area and going through the *Breaking Free* series on forgiveness by Beth Moore.

_____

_____

_____

_____

4. Have you accepted Jesus Christ as your personal Lord and Savior? If not, why not? What is holding you back from receiving all that Christ has and wants for you and your life?

_____

_____

_____

_____

Let's pray:

> Father God, I thank You for your faithfulness and patience with Your children. I pray for the one who has been abused and who uses this abuse to hate all peoples in a certain group. Please forgive us. Change our hearts to see all people as You see them. I ask it in Jesus's name. Amen.

Do I Have to Have a Relationship with My Abuser?

> If your brother sins against you, go and show him his fault, just between the two of you. If he listens to you, you have won your brother over. But if he will not listen, take one or two others along, so that "every matter may be established by the testimony of two or three witnesses." If he refuses to listen to them, tell it to the church; and if he refuses to listen even to the church, treat him as you would a pagan or a tax collector.
>
> Matthew 18:13–17

Jesus Himself said that if the person who abused you (committed sin against you) does not repent and refuses to be held accountable or take responsibility for his actions, then you are to treat him as a pagan or a tax collector. What does this mean? Well, in a nutshell, it means do not associate with him, do not have a relationship with him, and you certainly don't have to stay in contact with him. This was very comforting to me and, at the same time, very hurtful. I knew that if my parents refused to see the truth that I would end up losing them and would no longer be able to have a relationship with them. Unfortunately, this is exactly what happened, however, not by my choice. Let me explain.

God wired me with a gift for writing. I love to read and I love to write. I convey my thoughts, emotions, and feelings best when

I write. I am not a fast thinker when speaking, and I have to think about what I want to say before I say it.

This, by the way, was a direct result of the medication that I was placed on as a child that should have never entered my little body. The medication was given to me to "calm me down." It actually did damage to the part of the brain that controls cognitive thinking. I was never supposed to be on medication and the only reason both my brother and I were placed on this drug was so that our mother could watch her soap operas in peace and quiet.

I need to explain a little bit more about the medication my brother and I were placed on. My mother is a master manipulator and she can talk just about anyone into anything. She had the doctor convinced that my brother and I were completely unruly and needed to be "calmed down." This was not true. No testing, that I recall, was done on either myself or my brother to determine if, in fact, we needed to be on this drug. This, by the way, is a form of speed and allows a person who takes this as a child to be ten times more likely to abuse drugs as an adult.

A direct side effect of this drug resulted in the following: I think slower than most people, and my response time is slower as well. I express myself best through writing and can easily speak from the heart through this channel. This drug also stunted my growth. I am five feet five inches but should have been closer to six feet.

That being said, I wrote my mother a letter and attempted to explain to her the memories that had come back and that I remembered the truth of her abuse toward my brother and myself. At first she denied all of the abuse, claiming not to remember any of it. Then she came back and stated that children did not come with instructions and she did the best she could. Excuse me, while it is true enough that children do not come with instructions, parents have been equipped with a sense of discernment regarding right and wrong behavior toward children. God gives children as gifts to parents. Because of my mother's actions of abuse toward my brother and me, I was forced to grow up and become an adult at the age of seven.

The problem was that we never got the chance to be children! We were expected to be young adults—perfect in language, thought, word, and deed. Here is an example of this:

I was seven and my mother forced me to clean the bathroom with toxic cleaners in an enclosed small space with no ventilation. Remember, I was seven years old. I cleaned the bathroom as best as a seven-year-old could clean. After cleaning the bathroom with the toxic cleaners, my heart was palpitating, my hands were shaking, my stomach was upset, and I had a whopper of a headache—all due to the toxic cleaners my mother forced me to use. I thought that I had done a good job and was pretty proud of myself despite the ill side effects of the chemical cleaners. My mother came in to inspect my work. The next thing I knew, I was being yelled at for doing a horrible job and was beaten mercilessly with a belt across my bare skin because I had not cleaned the bathroom to her expectations, or in other words, like an adult. To this day, I do not clean bathrooms.

Another example of not being able to be a child is when we had company over. It didn't matter whether the company was family, i.e., grandparents, aunts, uncles, or cousins, or whether the company was my parents' friends or neighbors. My brother and I were, many times, ordered not to say one word or risk banishment to our bedrooms to be severely dealt with later. We were children! We were not allowed to act like children.

Thankfully, God has allowed me to be a child even though I am in my forties.

Luke 18:16 says, But Jesus called the children to him and said, "Let the little children come to me, and do not hinder them, for the kingdom of God belongs to such as these."

Since receiving Jesus as my Lord and Savior, I have my childlike qualities back. I am playful, naïve at times, and I look at the world around me with wonderment and awe.

My first letter to my mother did not get me anywhere, so I wrote another letter and then another and then another. I wasn't getting anywhere, so I suggested that my mother and I meet at a mutual location and talk about the truth. I met her at a local ice cream shop and, unbeknownst to us, they didn't open until noon! It was 9:00 a.m., and we were served ice cream! God was at work. We sat for five long hours in my mother's vehicle and talked. I poured my heart and soul out to her, asked lots of questions, and told her some of the sin that I did while in my rebellious stage as a teenager.

In short, I opened up to her like I never had before. I trusted her with very personal and confidential information. I trusted her to keep my confidence and not share what I had told her with anyone else. After that meeting, I felt good. I felt that we had aired everything out and now things would get better and maybe we could have the mother-daughter relationship that I longed for and desperately wanted. However, that was not to be. What I didn't realize then was that I had changed, but my mother had not. She still refused to accept responsibility for her actions, thoughts, words, and deeds. She had not repented and therefore had not changed.

After the marathon conversation, my cousins started asking me questions about certain issues I had confided in my mother about. This can't be! No! My mother would not have betrayed my confidence in what I had shared with her, would she? Oh yes. It was worse than that. Not only had she betrayed my confidence and told my aunt, uncle, and cousins what I had shared with her in deepest confidence and trust, but she boasted about it to them and even laughed at me for what I had shared with her. My trust was shattered, my heart was broken, again, and the mental abuse continued.

Off with another letter from me to her. I told her that my heart had been shattered by her gossiping lips and I demanded an apology. Do you know what I got? I received a letter from my father kicking me out of the family! I didn't think my heart could break anymore, nor did I think I could have been more deeply wounded. I was wrong.

I sought help from our pastor and my counselor. I was shaken to the core, and all that I had ever known had been ripped from me and I had been thrown away like garbage. This was the worst kind of pain I had ever known or experienced. Everything I had ever known and loved had been torn away, and I had been cast out of the only family I had ever known. My counselor explained to me that it was easier for my parents to disown me and throw me away than it was to acknowledge the truth and accept responsibility for their actions and be held accountable for the damage they had done. I was absolutely devastated. I threw myself into God's Word and walked away with Psalm 27 ringing in my ears:

> The LORD is my light and my salvation—whom shall I fear?
> · The LORD is the stronghold of my life—of whom shall I be afraid?
>
> When evil men advance against me to devour my flesh, when my enemies and my foes attack me, they will stumble and fall. Though an army besiege me, my heart will not fear, though war break out against me, even then will I be confident. One thing I ask of the LORD this is what I seek: that I may dwell in the house of the LORD all the days of my life, to gaze upon the beauty of the LORD and to seek him in his temple. For in the day of trouble he will keep me safe in his dwelling: He will hide me in the shelter of his tabernacle and set me high upon a rock. Then my head will be exalted above the enemies who surround me; at his tabernacle will I sacrifice with shouts of joy; I will sing and make music to the LORD. Hear my voice when I call, "O LORD; be merciful to me and answer me. My heart says of you, 'Seek his face!'" Your face, LORD, I will seek. Do not hide your face from me, do not turn your servant away in anger, you have been my helper. Do not reject me or forsake me. O God my Savior. *Though my father and mother forsake me, the Lord will receive me.* (Emphasis mine) Teach me your way, O LORD; lead me in a straight path because of my oppressors. Do not turn me over to the desire of my foes, for false witnesses rise up against me, breathing out violence. I am still confident of this: I will see the goodness of the LORD in the land of the living. Wait for the Lord; be strong and take heart and wait for the Lord.

Praise the Lord! Every time the enemy of our souls—satan—would place seeds of doubt that God did not love me or that I was not "honoring my mother and father," I would read the words of Psalm

27 and be comforted, knowing that God did love me and that He would never leave me or forsake me, but that He would protect me and receive me as His own child. A word of caution here: When you are down and hurting and have been cut to the very core, you are venerable. During these times in your life, you need to be especially careful and stay in God's Word or the enemy will try to deceive you and send you into despair and depression.

The main mission of satan is to destroy God's most precious creation: human beings. If he can get you down in such a state of despair, you might want to try killing yourself. So please be careful and surround yourself with a good Christian counselor, a pastor you trust, and God's Word.

My mother refused to honor my father's wishes and continued to contact me. I, again, sought help from my counselor and my pastor and God's Word. What I learned is this: My husband and I *were* honoring my father because we had obeyed my father's wishes in that we were not having any contact with the family. This is absolutely ridiculous when you look at it from the world's viewpoint. However, when you read what God has to say, you realize that we were honoring my father's wishes by staying away and it was my mother who was dishonoring her husband in continuing to contact us.

My mother didn't stop there; she invited us for Christmas and other holidays when my father had specifically stated he did not want us to be in his presence for any holiday or family gatherings. Talk about pouring salt in to a wound! This taunting behavior from my mother twisted the knife that was already tearing my heart to pieces. As of this date, I am convinced that my mother was just being cruel with her invitations when she knew that we would honor my father's wishes and stay away.

As you can imagine, this shattered my heart even more. I was so torn and my heart was damaged beyond just wounding. I loved my father so much and would comply with his wishes no matter how irrational and heart shattering they were. The only thing I was clinging to or knew was that God was and is in control and He was the only One that would be able to reach my father's heart and show my mother her disobedience. My father was in denial because he simply could not face the truth that his bride would turn into such a monster and abuse his children.

What you have to realize is that my mother is all about control and manipulation. She will do and say anything to justify her actions, refute the truth, deny the truth, and save face, i.e., her pride. After my father had disowned my husband and I and kicked us out of the family, we noticed that other family members were not contacting us. We did a little investigation and found out that my mother was gossiping about this situation, slandering our names, and making up lies about us in an attempt to justify her actions and make her and my father look innocent in their eyes. The saddest thing was not one family member came to us and asked if the lies were true. More painful was the fact that no one stood up to my mother and put her in her place for maliciously slandering us.

I confronted my mother through letters in an attempt to show her the damage she was causing. She completely ignored all of my letters and continued to justify her behavior and actions. You see, when my husband and I took control of our lives and took the control away from her, she resigned herself to get back, get even, take revenge, and punish us for not allowing her to control our lives in the very same way she controlled my father, grandparents, and brother's lives. How sad. My heart breaks for her to this day.

My husband and I did not defend ourselves or contact the people she had lied to in an attempt to change their minds. We know that God is in control and we know that the lies, gossip, and slander are known by God, and my mother knows what she has done to us. She will be held responsible and will have to answer for her actions to Almighty God. We wish her no ill will and harbor no revenge or hate in our hearts; rather, we have totally forgiven her because we know that she was listening to satan and not God, and God says to love and forgive and we obey.

Just because you forgive someone for wounding you, it does not mean that you have to have a relationship with that person. In the case of my mother, unless she completely repents and agrees to attend Christian counseling and agrees to go back and make things right by admitting her sin to our family and those she has lied to, we cannot have a relationship with her. There is no trust or respect, only forgiveness. As long as my mother refuses to be held accountable for her actions, there is no relationship because nothing in her has changed. It is not for us to make people who wound us change—that is God's job. We are to obey and forgive, pray for, and eventually love the people who wound us.

I know what you are thinking. How in the world can I forgive the person who wounded me? You have felt those wounds. Maybe you were raped by a stranger or someone familiar to you. Maybe you were beaten by parents, foster parents, or a bully at school. Maybe your spouse has abused you physically, mentally, or emotionally. Maybe you were slapped with divorce papers and never saw it coming. Maybe you were betrayed by a trusted pastor or friend. There are a zillion ways for people to wound and hurt us. Here is God's grace: when you can forgive that person, you are released from your anger, pain, and hate; then the healing can begin. When you can forgive, you will be able to come to a place where you can look at your abuser in a different light. This has happened for me and it can happen for you.

Hate the sin and not the person. Why? The reason is because there is a whole spiritual realm that we cannot see. At any given moment, we are either listening to God's voice and obeying Him, or we are listening to satan's voice and obeying him. We want to retaliate against the flesh because that is what we see. He hurt me! She hurt me! This was done to me by this person or that person. You can physically see the person who hurt you and that is what you want to hurt in return. What you can't see is the evil spirit—either satan or a demon of satan—whispering in his or her ear and justifying his or her actions. Let me give you an example of this. You have to go back to the beginning to see how this works.

Now the serpent was more crafty than any of the wild animals the LORD God had made. He said to the woman, "Did God really say you must not eat from any tree in the garden?" The woman said to the serpent, "We may eat fruit from the trees in the garden, but God did say, you must not eat fruit from the tree that is in the middle of the garden, and you must not touch it, or you will die." "You will not surely die," the serpent said to the woman. "For God knows that when you eat of it your eyes will be opened, and you will be like God, knowing good and evil."

Genesis 3:1

Do you see how satan works? He uses some truth with many lies to tempt you and me to do evil and sin against God.

So how does this relate to us today? Well, when my mother was abusing my brother and me, she would justify the abuse by stating that we did not come with instructions, we were bad and needed to be punished, and she was going to control her children and not allow her children to control her. See how satan used my mother to accomplish his will? See how he turned her heart away from God's commands, truth, and Word? If satan can convince your abuser that he or she is justified in his or her abuse toward you, then he can set into motion a chain of events that will ultimately destroy you if you do not turn to God and forgive that person. "The thief comes only to steal and kill and destroy; I have come that they may have life, and have it to the full" (John 10:10).

That is exactly what satan does. He convinces people to do evil and wound other people so that they will go after the flesh and hate and take revenge on that person. Do you see the cycle here? You hurt me; I hurt you; you retaliate; I retaliate. Can you see how satan can completely destroy lives by his lying and conniving? Ah, but you say that the abuser has a choice, that person can either listen or reject. Yes, that it true. God gave us all freewill. At that point, we have to go back to the cycle of sin. What in the abuser's past has led him or her to do the things that hurt you? Was that person abused? Chances are the answer is yes.

Someone has wounded you. You are hurt and hurting and you want to retaliate in the flesh. I know how you feel. I have been there. There was a time when I wanted to hurt and get back at my mother for everything she had done to me and to my brother. Then God gave me a very important piece to this puzzle and helped me understand.

He said in Ephesians 6:10–12, "For our struggle is not against flesh and blood, but against the rulers, against the authorities, against the powers of this dark world and against the spiritual forces of evil in the heavenly realms."

Did you get that? This is a huge piece to the forgiving process, when you can look at your abuser and realize that satan has control over that person. It is not the person you are warring against; it is satan!

Please hear me, my beloved friend, and get this truth way deep down into your heart. I know how you feel. I know your pain. I know how angry you are and I know you want justice. I did too and still do; only now I want God's justice, not mine. When you can look at the person who abused you and truly forgive him or her for the pain he or she has caused you and your loved ones, then you can realize that you are not fighting him or her; you are fighting the lord of this dark world.

———————————

God is light and love, mercy, gentleness, compassion, and grace. I love you and so does Jesus. I don't have to know you; I don't have to know what you have been through; I don't have to know your story to have compassion and love for you. I can say this because I have been abused and I know that pain. Give up your pain and live! Give up your revenge and live! Give all of your hurt and anger to God and allow Him to heal you. Do not take that poison any longer; give it to the One who can bring justice upon those who hurt you and wounded you so horribly.

———————————

Do you have to have a relationship with the person who abused you? No! Do you have to forgive that person? Yes. You have to forgive, but if there is not change in his or her life and he or she is toxic to you and your life, you do not have to have a relationship with him or her. It is not up to you to change that person or to make him or her see the sin that he or she has done. That is God's job. You are required to forgive that person, because it is not truly them you are warring against. It is satan and his demons that are causing all of the trouble.

This, then, is how you can come to love the person who hurt you. When you realize that he or she was listening to the wrong voice, you can pray for him or her. When you pray for him or her and have truly forgiven him or her in your heart and have truly released him or her to God, then God can and will show you how to love him or her. He will give you His love for that person who hurt you. He will love them through you, and as you allow God to love that person through you, you will realize that your wounds are healing and you are truly on the path to life!

Your wounds will heal. It may take time; it may take intensive counseling; it may take lots of tears and beating up innocent pillows, but you will heal and your wounds will be dressed by the love of Jesus Christ. Let Him heal you, beloved. He loves you so much and does not want you to hurt and hold all that pain inside. He wants you to release it to Him so He can deal with it. This is not your battle, my friend; it is God's battle, and it started way before you were ever a thought. God Almighty and satan have been battling ever since satan decided he wanted to be worshiped and wanted God's position. One of the best ways that satan can hurt and wound God is to attack His most treasured creation: human beings. And attack he does. So don't hold that anger inside; this is not your battle.

I want to explain what I mean by love your enemy or the person who hurt you. What exactly do I mean? When I say you can love your abuser I mean this: once you have forgiven the person who abused you from your heart, then you will no longer feel the rage, hate, anger, or any other negative emotions. You will no longer want revenge nor will you seek revenge against him or her. The perfect example I can show you of how you will come to love those who hurt you is the story of my favorite hero in the Bible, Joseph. You can read the whole story in Genesis starting in chapter thirty-seven and going through chapter fifty. It is a wonderful example of abuse and forgiveness, and I would strongly encourage you to read these chapters slowly and really create a picture in your mind of what is happening in each chapter. I did this and it really helped me to better understand the power of true forgiveness.

Joseph was sold into slavery by his brothers. His brothers hated him because he was his father's favorite child and he always got the best gifts, i.e., a colorful coat. His brothers were jealous of him and they decided to get rid of him. First, they threw him into a pit to die (I would imagine they roughed him up a bit first); then they sold him into Egyptian slavery.

Fast forward a bit and you come to the famine of Egypt and the surrounding areas. Joseph's brothers went to Egypt to beg for food for themselves and their father, Jacob. To wrap up my point, when the brothers finally realized Joseph was on the thrown and in charge, they were fearful of him and feared for their lives, assuming their brother, Joseph, would hurt or kill them for what they had done to him years before.

What did Joseph do? Did he sentence them to jail or prison or have them tortured or beaten? No. Did he order them to be killed? No. He certainly had the authority and power to do any of these things and worse. On his command, his guards would have taken care of those wicked brothers and Joseph would have had his revenge. No. When Joseph's brothers came to him begging for food (by the way, they didn't recognize him at first) and Joseph revealed himself to them, he came down from his thrown and fell on their necks and hugged them, kissing them and weeping. Does this sound like revenge to you? Would you or I have done the same thing?

If the person who abused you ever comes back into your life or is placed in front of you, then you will have to make a choice. You can either take out your anger and exact revenge on him or her or you can be like Joseph and tell him or her that you have forgiven him or her. Maybe you can't bring yourself to hug that person or weep on his or her neck, but you do not have to be unkind. Smile and tell him or her it is okay and he or she is forgiven. Then you will be loving that person and allowing Jesus to love him or her through you.

Just because you love your abuser and forgive him or her doesn't mean he or she can sweep everything under the rug and you become best buddies and pals. Remember, just because you have forgiven someone does not mean you have to have a relationship with him or her. You do not have to put yourself back in harm's way or allow yourself to be hurt by that person again. Maybe you simply walk away. That is okay too, but at least you rose to the occasion and allowed the Lord to love that person through you instead of exacting your revenge or treating him or her with disdain and hatred.

Here is another quick example of loving someone. Say you work in a financial institution and are in control of loaning money or you work as a police officer or you work in a restaurant. It doesn't matter what position, clout, or authority you hold. Now, you know your job well and one day the person who has hurt you deeply and crushed your heart comes in to see you for something. You have a choice. You can either come down hard on that person or use whatever authority you possess to inflict hurt upon him or her or you can treat him or her with dignity, respect, and compassion, showing that person love and no bitter or hard feelings. This may be a very tough choice at times, but I have faith that you can choose the right decision. I know; I have been there.

How do you think that person would respond to you? He or she knows what he or she has done to you; he or she knows how badly he or she has treated you and hurt you. Then that person gets in front of you, presumably asking for some type of help, goods, or service and you treat him or her with nothing but kindness and respect. I don't know about you, but if that were me and I had hurt someone and then that person was nice to me, I think it would blow my socks right off my feet! I would expect the worst and I would expect retaliation. Wouldn't you? By not retaliating against him or her and treating him or her with dignity and respect, you are showing him or her the love of Christ.

I am not justifying the abuse you suffered nor am I justifying the abuse I suffered. The people who abused you and me were listening to and following satan's voice and not the Savior's voice. That does not let them off the hook by any means. It simply means that we can forgive them, turn them over to God for His justice, and move on with our lives. We can even quite possibly come to love those people by allowing God to love them through us. As we pray, God will heal our wounds and time will allow us to move forward and the wounds of abuse will fade.

Let's review the facts:

1. You have been wounded by someone and the wounds are deep and they hurt. This person may be lying about the truth of your situation and attempting to make you look bad in an attempt to justify his or her own sin. Know this; you and God both know the truth. Hand that person over to God and completely forgive him or her so that you can get out of the way of God's justice.

2. The person who abused you may be toxic to you regardless of whether this person is a blood relation, friend, spouse, or stranger. If you have forgiven this person in your heart but that person shows no remorse or refuses to be held accountable for his or her actions and take responsibility for what he or she has done, then you *do not* have to have a relationship with that person.

3. Have nothing to do with this person! Keep him or her out of your life lest you fall and become like him or her if he or she has not repented and truly shown change in his or her life.

4. The evil one, satan, uses people and tries to tempt people into doing his will. God loves you and wants only what is best for you. We have a choice. At any given second or minute, we are either listening to and following satan or we are listening to and following God. When we can realize that the person who wounded us listened to satan and not God, we grow in our faith and understanding of the fact that we are not warring against flesh and blood, but against the evil forces that are at work. We want to retaliate against the flesh and blood because that is what we see with our eyes; use your spiritual eyes to see the truth.

Questions to Ponder

1. Have you truly forgiven the person who wounded you from your heart? Can you now hand that person over to God, knowing that He is a just and loving God? He will repay the evildoers in your life and you don't have to worry about revenge or making sure that your abusers get what they deserve.

2. Do you understand that you do not have to have a relationship with the people who abused you? Forgive them, yes; pray for them, absolutely. But you do not have to have a relationship with a person if he or she refuses to change, be held accountable for what he or she has done, and acknowledge and take responsibility for his or her actions.

_____

_____

_____

_____

3. Can you see that we are not fighting against flesh and blood? It was flesh and blood that wounded you, but it was satan's voice that commanded the abuse and not God's voice. By forgiving the person who abused you, you then give permission to God to take control of that situation. It is not up to you to force justice and take revenge—that is God's job and you are not God. I make no justifications for the abuser in your life. In order to truly survive and heal from that abuse, you must allow God to bring about justice. That may not be in your lifetime and that is where trust and faith come in.

_____

_____

_____

_____

Let's pray.

> Father God, it is difficult for us to pray for and forgive those who hurt us. Please help us and show us how to forgive those who have wounded us. Father, you are so faithful, and I would ask You to bless the people who are reading this book. Help them to let go of the anger and pain that drives revenge and hatred. Open their eyes to the truth of the spiritual world and the war that is going on around them. We lift this to You and ask it in Jesus's name. Amen.

Forgive Yourself

Then Jesus said to her, "Your sins are forgiven."

Luke 7:48

If you know your Bible, then you know about the woman at the Pharisee's house who anointed Jesus's feet with very expensive perfume, wiped His feet with her tears, and dried His feet with her hair. This woman had lived a sinful life, and she threw herself at the feet of Jesus to be forgiven. Jesus forgave her of her sins and told her that her faith had saved her and to go in peace. We don't know what the sins of this woman were, only that they were great and she had lived a very sinful life up to the point when she met Jesus.

My question to you is, if Jesus can forgive you of your sins—no matter what you have done, no matter what is in your past—then why can't you forgive yourself? That is a pretty powerful and loaded question. Too many times we think that our sin and what we have done are so great that God cannot possibly forgive us. This is simply not true. Let's go to another man who was a great sinner and see how Jesus handled him.

One of the criminals who hung there hurled insults at him: "Aren't you the Christ? Save yourself and us!" But the other criminal rebuked him, "Don't you fear God," he said, "since you are under the same sentence? We are punished justly, for we are getting what our deeds deserve. But this man has done nothing wrong." Then he said, "Jesus, remember me when you come into your kingdom." Jesus answered him, "I tell you the truth, today you will be with me in paradise."

Luke 23:39–43

The criminals who hung on the right and left of Jesus led sinful lives. We can plainly see this as the one criminal on the right admitted his sin and stated that they were getting what their deeds deserved. We don't know the details of their lives, only that they were being punished for their criminal deeds and their sin had finally caught up to them and they were now being punished and sentenced to die for their crimes against the people of that day.

If Jesus, hanging on the cross and dying a most painful and excruciating death, can forgive a man who had been a criminal probably all of his life, then He can forgive you! If Christ can forgive you of the most horrific sin, then you can forgive yourself. If you can't forgive yourself, then you call Jesus a liar, and you are, in effect, saying that you are above God and can justly rule against the sin in your life. This is sin itself. If Jesus says you are forgiven, then you are forgiven indeed! You are set free and you no longer have to be under the guilt and shame of your sinful deeds.

Second Corinthians 5:17 says, "Therefore, if anyone is in Christ, he is a new creation; the old has gone, the new has come." Once Jesus has forgiven you of your sins and you have repented, then you no longer have to live with the shame and condemnation of your past sin. The old has gone! No longer are you to dwell on your past sins; the new has come! Rejoice and be glad in Him that is Jesus, who has truly set you free! And if the Savior, Jesus Christ, has set you free, then you are free indeed! Before I had accepted Christ as my Savior and Lord of my life, I was a rebellious sinner. I am still a sinner and that will not change until I am face-to-face with Jesus, but I have been set free of my former and past sins. When Jesus died on the cross, He forgave all sin—past, present, and future. When He died on that cross, He was dying for your sin and my sin. We weren't even born yet, but He knew the sin that would invade our lives and cause us to wander away from God's Word, morals, and values for our lives.

When we accept Jesus as our Lord and Savior, we are sealed with the Holy Spirit so that when God Almighty looks at us, He sees His beloved Son and not our sins. That is what it means to be covered in the blood of Jesus. Jesus died for us and took our sin upon Him at the cross so that we could have a restored relationship with the Creator, our God, the God of Abraham, Isaac, and Jacob.

I was very much like the Samaritan woman at the well when Jesus found me. The story of the Samaritan woman goes like this: Jesus was thirsty and tired. He had to go through Samaria and came to a town called Sychar, which was near the plot of ground that Jacob had given to his son, Joseph. Jacob's well was there and Jesus sat down by the well. Let's pick up the story as recorded in John 4:7–18:

> When a Samaritan woman came to draw water, Jesus said to her, "Will you give me a drink?" (His disciples had gone into town to buy food.) The Samaritan woman said to him, "You are a Jew and I am a Samaritan woman. How can you ask me for a drink?" (For Jews did not associate with Samaritans.) Jesus answered her, "If you knew the gift of God and who it is that asks you for a drink, you would have asked Him and He would have given you living water." "Sir," the woman said, "you have nothing to draw with and the well is deep. Where can you get this living water? Are you greater than our father, Jacob, who gave us the well and drank from it himself, as did also his sons and his flocks and herds?" Jesus answered, "Everybody who drinks this water will be thirsty again, but whoever drinks the water I give him will never thirst. Indeed, the water I give him will become in him a spring of water welling up to eternal life." The woman said to him, "Sir, give me this water so that I won't get thirsty and have to keep coming here to draw water." He told her, "Go call your husband and come back." "I have no husband," she replied. Jesus said to her, "You are right when you say you have no husband. The fact is, you have had five husbands, and the man you now have is not your husband. What you have just said is quite true."

I have to believe that Jesus forgave this woman of her sin and she believed in Him the rest of her days. We are not told this in the Bible, but we are told that the woman left her jar at the well and ran to town to tell the people of the man who had told her all about herself and her past. That fact alone is amazing. She ran to town. The woman came to draw water from the well when no one else would be there! She avoided other people like the plague and now she was running to town to tell them about her encounter with Jesus! Talk about change! She had an encounter with the King and that can never leave you the same as you were before meeting Him.

Like I said, I was very much like this woman at the well. Jesus gently and lovingly confronted me about my past relationship with guys I had gone after prior to my marriage to my husband; He showed me how I attempted to find "living water" or true love. I desperately wanted to be loved. I was also looking for a protector. I didn't learn this until much later when I went through the *Open Hearts* and *Breaking Free* Bible studies.

Now back to forgiving myself. I had sinned big time! I had not repented of the sexual immorality I had committed against God prior to marrying my husband. I knew I had messed up big time, and I felt the weight of the guilt and shame. I really didn't like myself all that much and I certainly had no use for other people, regardless of whether they were kind or not. I loved my husband and extended family, but that was about it. I had been let down so many times that my trust in others was shattered and my respect for the human race, in general, was nonexistent.

What I have learned is that people who have been abused usually don't have a high self-esteem or confidence in themselves. If you don't love yourself, you are virtually incapable of loving others. This became true of me. The hardest part for me was to forgive myself.

After I had forgiven my mother and accepted Jesus as my Lord and Savior that November day, God started prompting me to forgive myself. I was going deeper with God and was learning and reading about Him as fast as I could. I wanted to know this awesome God I had just put my faith in. He wanted me to know that He knew me since before the beginning of time and that He formed me in my mother's womb. But forgive myself? How? Why? I didn't deserve to be forgiven. Well, that may be true but the thief on the cross dying with Jesus didn't deserve to be forgiven either. Jesus forgave the thief and He forgave me and was calling me to forgive myself.

Yes, you can forgive yourself. I have forgiven myself, and the peace that lives in my heart is definitely not of this world. I was ugly in thought, word, and deed, but Jesus Christ forgave my sins and took all of my shame and guilt. He has shown me love, mercy, and grace. He has turned my ashes into beauty, my sadness into gladness.

Let me share with you what will happen when you come to the place of forgiving yourself. I am speaking from experience here. I forgave my mother and the other people who had hurt me. God showed me that I could no longer have a relationship with my mother because there was no support or love there, only a desire to exact revenge, control, and manipulate me. This is not God's will for my life, and if someone is doing this to you, it is not God's will for your life either.

Remember the marathon conversation I told you about that I had with my mother? I told her some very private and confidential things that I had not shared with anyone else. I trusted her with my most personal heartaches and sin and trusted her not to expose this information to any other person and betray my trust. Well, after I had forgiven myself, my mother saw in me that I had no guilt, shame, anger, hate, or rage. All of that had been taken away by Jesus. I had truly let the past die and I was moving forward in freedom and with a new love and compassion for other people.

I have to believe that my mother was envious of my newfound freedom and she wanted it for herself but didn't know how to get it. In my mother's mind, the only logical thing to do since she didn't know how to obtain this freedom in Christ was to attempt to bring me back to the guilt and shame so that I would be back in bondage and chains. In other words, if she didn't know how to receive this freedom, then she felt her daughter shouldn't be free either.

Why am I sharing this with you? Because this type of behavior could come your way when you forgive yourself. There will be people in your life who will be envious of your newfound freedom in Christ. They will want your peace, your joy, your happiness, your love, and they won't know how to get this if they don't truly know Christ. They will accuse you of being self-righteous, prideful, and maybe even snobbish. Rest assured you are not! Once Jesus gives you the peace and you have truly accepted the forgiveness from Jesus, then you can forgive yourself and leave the past in the past and move forward.

I want to give you a word of warning here. Just because you have forgiven yourself does not mean you can go on deliberately sinning.

Romans 6:1–4 states: "What shall we say, then? Shall we go on sinning so that grace may increase? By no means! We died to sin: how can we live in it any longer? Or don't you know that all of us who were baptized into Christ Jesus were baptized into His death? We were therefore buried with Him through baptism into death in order that, just as Christ was raised from the dead through the glory of the Father, we too may live a new life."

Just because you are forgiven and have forgiven those who hurt you and have forgiven yourself does not mean you can continue in your old sinful lifestyle.

What does this mean? Well, if you used to sleep around, stop it! If you used to lie, stop it! If you used to steal, stop it! Whatever Jesus has forgiven you for and you have repented of, you need to turn from that sin lifestyle and move forward. I am not saying you won't fall every now and again, but the thought is that Jesus forgave you of your sins; don't slap Him in the face and deliberately continue to sin. Yes, He has forgiven you and He loves you, but don't tempt the Lord your God lest you experience His wrath upon you and your life.

You may not be able to kick those old bad habits overnight. You may have to have help in stopping the sin that has infested your life. I would suggest you pray to God and ask Him to help you stop sinning. It may take time, but if you continually pray about it, He is just and will help you to eventually turn from that sin.

You will want to remain humble. If you treat people better than yourself, it will be hard for pride to sneak in and it will be hard for you to become righteous in your own eyes. Remember the sins that God has forgiven you of and thank and praise Him! Ask Him for His help in helping you to turn from your sinful ways. It won't be easy. Old habits die hard, and it is really easy to slip back into old patterns and ways of thinking.

Remember, you are a new creation in Christ. The old is gone; the new is here! Rejoice in the new and put away old ways of doing things. Paul said in Romans 6:14, "For sin shall not be your master, because you are not under law, but under grace."

Grace covers a multitude of sins, but this does not mean you can go on sinning. You must stop, and if you can't, then you must ask God for help.

An amazing thing happens when you learn to forgive yourself. You start to like yourself, maybe for the first time in your life, like me. I never really liked or loved myself. I wanted to die. I couldn't handle the abuse anymore. If this was all there was to life, I didn't want any part of it. I would take my chances on the other side of this life. I am thankful now that God allowed me to live. I would have missed out on too much. When you start to love yourself and accept yourself for who God made you to be, then you can start to love other people.

Until you love and accept yourself, however, don't expect to love or have the ability to love someone else. It just won't happen. You can try to convince yourself that you love someone, but when you get right down to it and search your heart, you will find that you really don't love other people. It will come out as anger, noncompassion, irritation, lack of patience, and other negative emotions.

I used to work with a young lady who did not know the Lord. We played the same role at the judicial job I had. I attempted to explain to her it was not our job to continue to carry out judgment on people or make his or her life more miserable. Our job was to help the person who committed the crime to pay his or her debt to society by enforcing the rules the Judge had set forth as punishment. I explained that we did not need to be rude or nasty with the people who came into our office or to set the bar so high that they would fail. She made a comment to me one day that she was trying to have compassion on people. You can't try to have compassion on people; either you do or you don't. What she was really saying is that she didn't love herself, didn't believe in God, had no relationship with Jesus Christ, and was incapable of loving or having compassion on anyone, including herself. I tried to show her the love of Jesus by showing her how I worked with the criminals who came through our door. I was kind, compassionate, and tried to show them that just because they had committed a crime against society didn't mean they couldn't be forgiven or given a second chance, but she told me that all people had to do was play the "Christian card" and I would melt and relent and give them special treatment or favor. She truly doesn't know the Lord and the wonderful grace and mercy she could receive from Him. What she didn't understand is that I treat all people the same regardless of whether they have been kind to me or not and regardless of whether they are a Christian or not.

God is no respecter of persons, so why should I be? People take the Lord's name in vain, raise their angry fists and shake them in His face, and treat Him with contempt, and the Lord still loves them. So who am I to treat people who don't like me any different from those who love me? Hard concepts to get your mind around, I know. But spend some time in God's Word and in prayer with the Father and He will change your heart and the way you look at people.

What we have to remember is that there is evil in this world. Unfortunately, satan is alive and well and roams around like a lion looking for people to devour. Part of learning to forgive you is to see people in a different light.

> For our struggle is not against flesh and blood, but against the rulers, against the authorities, against the powers of this dark world and against the spiritual forces of evil in the heavenly realms.
>
> Ephesians 6:12

We do not war against the people who have wounded us; we war against the enemy of God, that is satan and his band of demons. They are the ones who put evil thoughts into the minds of people and twist the truth of God's Word. People are like sheep and can be led astray so very easily. Don't believe me? Take a look at peer pressure. If one kid jumps off the dock, then all of them will follow. Same goes for adults.

If your co-workers are going to the local pub after work for a drink, watch how many people will follow them. If you follow them, then you are considered among the in crowd; if you don't, then you are an outcast and treated as such. As followers of Christ, we need to stand up and follow Him and not the crowds. When you are a follower and believer in Christ, you are set apart from the crowd.

So what does this have to do with forgiving yourself? Well, if you forgive yourself, you will have a confidence that is not yours. You will have God's confidence that He loves you, cares for you, will provide for and protect you, and He will give you the strength, wisdom, and discernment to either follow the crowd or recognize that following the crowd is not a good idea. He gives you the strength to say, "No. I can't follow the crowd to the local pub because I have a wife or husband at home, and God would want me to go home to my family rather than drink alcohol in a stinky pub where there is temptation and potential disaster."

Now, you may be shunned at work, but if you are working for God, who cares? Jesus tells us that if they persecuted Him, they will persecute you for following Him. You have to remember that you are a representative of Christ if you are a follower of Him. If you are seen in a bar or local drinking establishment, what kind of message are you sending to the people who don't know God? Where is the difference between you and them?

————————————

Hopefully, by now you realize how much God loves you and how much He wants to rid you of your guilt and shame that is a result of your sin. One last thing I would tell you: please hear me on this, my friend, for it will be the hardest thing you will have to hear and then do. You can cry out to God to forgive you of your sins. God will forgive you; however, the meaning of repent is to change. You must turn from your wicked ways and allow God to transform your heart. Part of that process is making the wrongs you have done right.

What do I mean by that? Well, let's go to Scripture again and let the Word of God explain. The story of Manasseh, king of Judah, and son of Hezekiah, king of Israel, sinned against God and he did much wickedness in the sight of the Lord. The Lord tried to speak to Manasseh, but he was not listening, so God allowed this king to be captured by his enemies. King Manasseh's enemies put a hook through his nose, bound him with bronze shackles, and took him to Babylon.

> In his distress, he sought the favor of the LORD his God and humbled himself greatly before the God of his fathers. And when he prayed to him, the LORD was moved by his entreaty and listened to his plea; so he brought him back to Jerusalem and to his kingdom. Then Manasseh knew that the LORD is God.
>
> 2 Chronicles 33:12–13

That is not the end of it. Just because Manasseh repented and cried out to God and had his sins forgiven, there was more required of him. King Manasseh had to make the wrongs that he did right. So what did he do?

> He got rid of the foreign gods and removed the image from the temple of the LORD, as well as all the altars he had built on the temple hill and in Jerusalem, and he threw them out of the city.
>
> 2 Chronicles 33:15

Do you see what happened here? You must go back and make it right for as much of that is in your control. If you have lied about someone, gossiped about someone, or slandered someone's name and you know that what you have said and done is not the truth, you must go back and make the wrongs right. That is very painful and it may cost you respect and trust of others, but you will be vindicated in God's eyes and you will find favor with Him. If you simply repent and not make the wrongs right, as much as it is up to you, then you will be forgiven but may not receive the favor or blessings of God.

Again, I am speaking from experience here. I used to exaggerate and say things that made me, I thought, look important. I have had to go back and admit that I never met the famous people I claimed to have met. I understand why I said the things I said. My self-esteem and confidence were so low I truly believed no one would like or even love me just the way I am. What I claimed was wrong and was sin. I make no excuses for my exaggerations. I have repented and lamented to God, but it wasn't until I went back and admitted to the people I had told this to that I found favor and blessing from God. It was painful. I did lose a little bit of trust and respect, but I have worked hard at turning from this sin and have regained the trust and respect I lost. By going back and setting the wrongs you have done right, you help yourself to grow, and this works as a great deterrent to not slip back into old habits and repeat the same sin.

It is never easy to admit when you are wrong and have sinned. Pride is ugly and it can consume you if you are not careful. In James 4:6, we read in part, "God opposes the proud, but gives grace to the humble."

===

My goal was to give you a broad picture for forgiving yourself and to show you all aspects of your life that will be affected. Jesus told us that it is a hard life following Him and that is true; however, it is the best life, and when you have that peace that surpasses all under-standing, you can stand at the gates of hell, look the devil in the eye, and laugh at him because you have Jesus Christ as your Lord and Savior. You will live eternally with Him, and you can live on this earth knowing that whatever life throws at you, you are loved by the Most High God, the God of Abraham, Isaac, and Jacob, the one true living God. Rejoice and be glad in this day! Give God praise and sing to Him songs of praise because the King has set you free and you are free indeed!

You can forgive yourself, God can heal your wounds, and He will forgive you. For your part, you need to go back, if it is at all in your power, and make the wrongs that you have done right. God will most assuredly do His part and forgive you if you truly repent and admit your sin to Him, but He will expect you to take care of the harm from the effects your sin has caused other people. He will expect you to go back and make the wrongs you have done right.

Finally, is there someone who has come to you and asked for your forgiveness? What was your response? Anytime anyone asks you for your forgiveness for what he or she has done to you, you must forgive. It makes no difference what the hurt was; you need to forgive the sin and allow the person to come clean. Jesus said that He would forgive us as we forgive others.

What does it mean when Jesus said we will be forgiven as we forgive others? Just exactly that. It is very simple. Jesus died on the cross for all of us, for all sin, for all of the sin people commit against each other. If Jesus, dying on the cross, can forgive me of lying, sexual immorality, wanting to die, wanting to exact revenge, then who am I to say that I refuse to forgive someone who comes to me and asks for my forgiveness for his or her sin against me? In effect, what Jesus is saying is that if someone comes to us and asks us to forgive him or her for hurting us and we say, "I'm sorry, but what you have done to me is just too great, and I am incapable of ever letting that hurt go, and I cannot forgive you," then He cannot forgive you for sinning against Him, the Father, or the Holy Spirit.

I would like to give you a quick example of this. David Berkowitz was formerly known as the *Son of Sam*. He murdered people back in the sixties and seventies. He was caught, convicted, and sentenced to life in prison without parole. While in prison, he met a man who led him to Jesus Christ. David eventually turned his life over to Christ, repented of his sins, and asked forgiveness for those families he had destroyed by killing a loved one. David then turned to the families and asked forgiveness from them for killing someone they loved. He said he was not asking to be paroled, was not asking to be set free; he acknowledged that he had committed horrible atrocities against good families, and he was only asking that they forgive him for hurting them so deeply by taking the life of someone they loved. Their response was not his issue. Their response was between them and God.

God says to those families, "I know you have been wounded and hurt, and I know this man wrongfully and maliciously stole the life of someone you desperately loved and cared for. I understand that, and it is My justice that will be done to this man for what he has done. I alone will righteously judge this man and repay evil for evil as I see fit, and I expect you to forgive this man because I have forgiven you (if they have repented and accepted Jesus as their personal Lord and Savior) of all of the sin you have committed against Me, the Father and Holy Spirit." What is hard for us to get our mind around is the fact that God can love someone who hurt us so deeply and then ask us to give up our worldly right to justice, revenge, and total payback so that we might be able to feel better and feel somewhat justified that we have carried out the proper sentence, in our eyes, for that person.

The bottom line in forgiving someone who is asking you or me to forgive the sins he or she committed against you or me is that Jesus will judge and forgive us as we have forgiven those who have sinned against and wounded us. It is one thing to forgive someone who doesn't ask us for forgiveness; it is something all together different when someone asks us to forgive and we refuse. Not much else will send the wrath of God upon you faster than refusing to forgive someone who is asking for your forgiveness.

My personal opinion is that it takes a lot for someone to humble himself, set aside his pride, admit that he was wrong, acknowledge that wrong, and then ask you to forgive him. There is no sin that is committed against us that cannot be forgiven just as there is no sin that you can commit that God cannot forgive. The only exception to this would be the sin of grieving the Holy Spirit by refusing to acknowledge that Christ is the only begotten Son of God and accepting His free gift of salvation for your life.

I include this language in my daily prayer to Jesus every day: "Father God, please forgive me of (I list all of the known sin I have committed during that day), as I have forgiven those who have deeply wounded, abused, betrayed, and hurt me. I forgive my mother, father, my former stepfather-in-law and his sister and brother-in-law, my aunt and uncle and cousins who have thrown me away because they listened to the lies of satan spewed out from the mouth of my mother. Father, I ask that you forgive each of them and lead them into a relationship with You and help them to accept the free gift of eternal salvation only available through Your Son, Jesus Christ, that they may experience the love and forgiveness that you have shown me."

I wasn't always able to pray this prayer and mean it. There was so much pain and hurt I had to let go of. It took a long time of continually handing over that pain and exposing the wounds they inflicted upon me to God. I had to let go and let God. That is the hard part. We don't want to give up our own control to make the wrongs done to us right, but we must if we want peace, grace, and blessings to flow over us. Instead we must walk away and allow God to heal wounds, restore relationships, and allow forgiveness on all fronts to rule the day. Rest assured, God will put the wrongs done to you right, and He will restore to you a double portion of all that you lost in His time and in His way. Be patient, stay in faith and in the Word, and trust God for the results.

Let's review the facts:

1. The greater the sin in a person's life, the greater the peace and grace you receive once you repent of your sins and accept Jesus Christ as your Lord and Savior. No matter what you have done in your life, God can and eagerly waits to forgive you. God loves you, but you have freewill. You can choose life through Jesus Christ or you can choose death; even if you don't make a choice, you still have made a choice. This is called

freewill and God will not force you to choose Him. He wants you to choose Him but won't force you.

2. Forgive yourself and experience God's peace, grace, mercy, and love in your life. Remember the woman at the well? She was full of sin and Jesus knew it, but He forgave her and loved her right where she was. If God can forgive you for your sin, you can forgive yourself. No longer dwell in the shame and guilt of what you have done, but let the blood of Christ cover you. That is why He died for you on the cross—to take upon your sin so you would not have to live with it any longer. Give it to Him. He is ready and willing to take it from you and forgive you and show you love like you have never known.

3. Once you have accepted God's forgiveness of your sins, you must go back and make the wrongs right. Inasmuch as it depends upon you or is in your control, you must go back and admit to the people what you have done. Chances are they have already forgiven you if they are walking with the Lord. However, their response to your admissions is not your issue nor is it within your control. You are simply obeying God and making the wrongs you have done right. The response is between God and that person.

Questions to Ponder

1. Do you have unrepented sin in your life? Have you asked God to forgive you? Once God forgives you, are you then able to forgive yourself?

_____

_____

_____

_____

2. Have you sinned against someone in thought, word, or deed? Have you lied about someone, spread gossip and slander that you either knew was not true or that just came from your own speculation and thoughts? Have you gone back to that person and asked for forgiveness, admitting what you have said or done? Remember, his or her response is not in your control. That is between that person and God. God is calling you to obey and make the wrongs in your life right; obey and feel His love and grace and watch for His hand of favor and blessing to be upon you.

_____

_____

_____

_____

3. Finally, is there someone who has come to you and asked for your forgiveness? If so, what was your response? Did you accept his or her apology or did you tell that person you couldn't forgive him or her? If you said or did anything that did not reflect the love of Christ, then you will need to go back to that person and apologize. God's wrath will be upon those who have been forgiven and yet refuse to forgive those who wounded them.

_____

_____

_____

_____

Let's pray:

Father God, thank You for the gift of forgiveness through Your Son, Jesus Christ. Thank You for His work on the cross to forgive us of our sins against You. Father, You call us to forgive one another and You expect us to make the wrongs we have committed against others right. Please help us. It is hard for us to lay down our pride and admit to someone else that we have lied or done something to hurt another person. Please bring any unrepented sin to our minds now so that we may repent and turn from our wicked ways. Help us to trust in You alone and not care what other people think of us. For it is You alone that we serve and not man. We give you all the praise and Glory and ask it in Jesus's name. Amen.

How Many Times Do I Have to Forgive?

Then Peter came to Jesus and asked, "LORD, how many times shall I forgive my brother when he sins against me? Up to seven times?" Jesus answered, "I tell you, not seven times, but seventy-seven times."

Matthew 18:21–22

How many times, Lord, do I have to forgive my mother? Over and over again, I hear the gossip and lies and slander that she is saying about my husband and I. I want so badly to make her stop. How many times, Lord, do I forgive my mother for turning the family, people in our church, and my husband's bosses against us with her slander and lies? How many times, Lord ... well, you get the point. Who do you know that constantly sins against you? Maybe someone who is always trying to get you into trouble, maybe a boss or co-worker or a sibling? How many times should we forgive? How long do we have to put up with this?

So many times I have asked God that question, and the words of Jesus come back to me from Matthew: "I tell you, not seven times (or ten or fifteen or twenty times) but seventy-seven times." Isn't that a hard truth to hear? It is for me. My immediate response is that I want to make them stop hurting me. Stop lying! Stop gossiping! Stop slandering my husband's good name! What is wrong with you? Why can't you see the damage you are doing?

Have you ever felt this way? Who in your life is constantly putting you down, saying and doing things that really hurt you, damage you, and leave a bitter taste in your mouth? Maybe it is someone who embarrasses you in front of other people or puts you down in some hurtful way. The examples and situations are endless.

Our natural human flesh response is to get back at that person or make him or her stop the activity he or she is doing that hurts us. What we have to realize, again, is that we do not war against flesh and blood. We are warring against satan and his demons, and the battle really is not ours. Once we can wrap our minds around the truth of the spiritual realm of our existence, then it becomes easier to understand the wickedness and evil people do.

This in no way excuses the person or his or her actions, thoughts, words, and deeds toward us. This person has a conscience and he or she has the ability to distinguish between right and wrong. It is his or her choice and, quite frankly, before I met Jesus, I actually enjoyed hurting others. Sick but true. The reason is because when I was hurting other people and making them feel bad, I didn't feel so bad about myself. Sin does horrific things to our minds and bodies. If you have seen the movie *The Lord of the Rings*, then you can get a very real picture of what sin does to us.

There is a character in one of my favorite movies that has two distinct personalities: one good and one bad, or depicted as sin. All the evil and sin its bad side had made the creature become quite an ugly thing. It is a very good depiction of what sin, if left unchecked, can do to us.

In contrast, since I have received Jesus as my Lord and Savior and have decided to follow Him, people have come up to me and said that I glow. I am not quite sure what they mean by that, but I have to believe that they are not seeing me but rather the light and love of the Holy Spirit who lives within me.

It is sad when you can walk through a crowd and pretty much tell who is lost and dead in their sins and those who have given their lives to Christ. It is almost like night and day. May I suggest to you that if you encounter someone who truly is lost and does not know the Lord, pray for that person right where you are and in that moment. Just close your eyes, if possible, and lift that person up to the Lord and ask

Him to open his or her blind eyes and unlock his or her deaf ears. You never know whose life you will affect by doing this.

━━━━━━━━━━

To forgive just one time and be done with it is not realistic nor is it what God has called us to do. People are human creatures and their flesh or nature is to sin. Not one person is perfect and we will never be able to escape sin until we are in the glorious presence of the Lord where our earthly bodies will be changed to a glorified body like the risen Christ. I, for one, can't wait!

Ask yourself a question. Once you have received Jesus as your personal Lord and Savior, are you done sinning once and for all? No! You can't be. It is impossible. The Lord can help you turn from your obvious evil sinful ways, but it is a process and you will need His help to accomplish this. You will never be able to get rid of all the sin in your life until you are in the presence of the Lord. What is my point?

Well, if you know that you won't be perfect and without sin until you meet the Lord, then you also know that the person who has wounded you won't be able to rid him or herself of his or her sin nature either. If you know this, then you can understand why Jesus said we need to keep on forgiving. He knew no one would be perfect or sin free after he or she accepted Him as his or her Lord and Savior. He knew that whoever wounded you would continue to do so unless and until He was able to change them.

Now, the flip side to this is that, yes, you need to forgive people every time they hurt and wound you. That does not mean you have to have a relationship with a toxic person.

My mother abused us as children, as explained in the first chapter of this book. At first, she did not admit to the abuse; then she admitted the abuse but gave many justifications and excuses for her actions. Once the physical abuse had ceased, she turned to mental, emotional, and spiritual abuse in an attempt to control us. After I got married, this type of abuse continued. I was trying to "leave and cleave" to my husband, but my mother was trying to control me as if

I were fourteen years old and still living under her roof. My mother has a control issue and a letting go issue. What she didn't understand is that children are a gift from God. Parents are required to nurture the personality God placed within the child and to raise them and protect them but then allow them to go and be what God has called them to be and to serve Him. My mother wanted to mold us in to what she wanted us to do and be when we grew up and not what God wanted for us.

My husband and I started a new sales business, wherein we were trying to sell organic supplements in an attempt to have better health. I have already told you the story in a previous chapter, so I won't go over it again. The point is that my mother attended my "infomercial" as the devil's advocate. She put down the products at every turn and asked demeaning questions of my hosts. There was no support or love for me or my husband or for what we were trying to promote. I had been physically healed by these products and I have a very powerful testimony with respect to them. I wanted to help other people feel and have the same positive affects of these products like I had. We were not looking to get rich; we were looking to help people have healthier bodies.

My mother has not given us any type of support for any job, business, or decision we have ever made. She is constantly putting down our thoughts, ideas, or plans. She is constantly spewing forth negative comments and criticisms about our home, our jobs, our taste in music, and even our church. This is toxic behavior. Please hear me here. I love my mother. I love my father. They are 100 percent totally forgiven, and I have absolutely no hate, anger, rage, or negativity toward them. I feel pain and am wounded by their behavior, but I continue to forgive them time and again, unconditionally, through the help of Jesus. The point is you can't have a relationship with someone who is constantly negative, does not support anything you do or say, and does not provide love or space. This is a toxic person.

Do you see the difference here? Do I want a relationship with my parents? Yes! Absolutely! The fact of the matter is that when you are constantly around someone who is always putting you down or speaking negatively about your surroundings, ideas, plans, home, etc., this will bring you down. It is painful and it hurts. It wounds us deeply and we have to stay away; this is called putting up boundaries. We have to put up barriers or boundaries to prevent ourselves from being led astray.

Nothing would make me happier than if my mother and father accepted responsibility for the damage they have done and allowed God to hold them accountable for their thoughts, words, and deeds. I have asked them to attend Christian counseling with my husband and me, but they have refused. The bottom line is they refuse to acknowledge and accept responsibility for their actions, they refuse to repent of their sin, and they refuse to take any steps toward reconciliation. My heart breaks for them. The sad truth is they are so full of pride that they cannot afford to lose face with all the people they have talked to about my husband and me. People like this are toxic and refuse to change or allow God to show them their need for repentance and change.

I have been betrayed over and over again and God has shown me that these people are not to be trusted, even if they are flesh and blood family.

———

Whenever word gets back to me of something my mother has said, I have to check my anger and immediately forgive her; giving the lie, slander, or gossip to God and releasing it from my heart. Sometimes it is hard not to hate my mother, but God always gives me the strength and courage to turn the other cheek. He reminds me through Scripture that I am to forgive as He forgave me, that I am warring against satan and his demons and not the flesh and blood of my mother and that I can do all things through Him who strengthens me. Sometimes it is difficult. I want to hang on to that anger. When people wound us, we want to be angry with them and we are justified in the world's eyes for doing so, but that is not what God calls us to do. He says, "Forgive seventy-seven times."

─────────────────

How about you? Is there a person in your life who just gets under your skin? Can you forgive him or her again and again and as many times as it takes? It is not easy. Have you ever said you would not forgive someone if he or she did that one more time? That is not of God. That is sin. Jesus commands that we forgive and forgive and forgive, and the reason is because that is exactly what Jesus did for you and for me on the cross. It goes right back to our sin natures. Have you stopped sinning because you were saved? No. I can guarantee it. You may have changed some bad habits or allowed the Lord to change your heart toward people, but you still sin from time to time. I know I do, and I know there are no perfect or sinless people on this earth. So chance are you have sinned, maybe even this morning.

When Jesus died for our sins, He died for the ones past, present, and future. Let me say that again. Jesus died for your sins and my sins from the past (what we were and what we did before accepting Christ), the present (the sins we commit on a daily basis, those both known and unknown), and future (those sins that we will commit in the future that we don't even know about now).

How many sins did Jesus forgive? All of them. How many sins committed against us should we forgive? All of them. Even the ones committed over and over again? Yes, all of them. Do you see a pattern here? Jesus forgave all of your sins, and He commands us to forgive all the sins committed against us.

I can almost hear your thoughts: *You just don't know what he/she/ they did to me.* No, I don't. True enough. I don't know what horrific things were done to you, but I am sure that it broke your heart or shattered your dreams or wounded you very deeply. I am sorry that you ever had to go through that. My heart bleeds for you, but that is exactly the reason I have written this book: to help people who have suffered at the hands of others. My friend, I am speaking to you through experience here. I know your pain. I know your desire for revenge and your want to strike back and hurt them as much as they hurt you. I am not the one who is asking you to forgive; God is. Jesus tells us in Matthew 18:35: "This is how my heavenly Father will treat each of you unless you forgive your brother from your heart."

What is He talking about here? Just before that passage in Scripture, Jesus tells a story of two servants. One servant owes his master a lot of money (millions of dollars), but he pleads with his master and his master forgives him his debt. Then the forgiven servant goes out and finds a fellow servant who owes him a little money (maybe a few thousand bucks) and practically chokes him and demands that this guy pay up or else. Well, the master heard what had happened after he had forgiven his servant much and got really angry. He turned the forgiven servant over to the jailers to be tortured until he paid back all he owed. Ouch! And then Jesus says that this is how our heavenly Father will treat us if we fail to forgive someone who sins against us. That is reason enough for me! As we forgive others, this is how God will forgive us. This leads me to a very interesting example of the story Jesus told.

My husband and I have a very dear friend we love very much. She is very sick and is playing a very dangerous game with her faith. She claims to believe in Jesus and claims that He is her Savior and Lord. However, her actions do not line up with her words. She had a relationship with a man and was living with him for many years. This guy borrowed a lot of money from our friend and was into drugs and partying and gambling. They ended up terminating their relationship and going their separate ways.

The guy in this story has truly given his life to Christ and has turned his life around. He is now married to a godly woman and he no longer does drugs or gambles like he used to. For his part in the relationship, this guy completely forgave our friend for the pain she caused him and has repented of the pain and suffering he caused her.

In contrast, our friend has not forgiven this guy for hurting her. We have talked to her about forgiveness, but she claims to have made a peace about it. No. You don't make a peace about forgiveness. Either you forgive the person that hurt you or you don't. There is no middle ground, no gray area. It is black and white. It is along the same lines of *you are married or not; either you are pregnant or you are not*. You get the idea here. You have either forgiven someone for the hurt and pain they caused you or you haven't.

The difference between our two friends is like night and day. Remember me telling you about a little creature in one of my favorite movies that had two distinct personalities? Well, that is our friend. She is sick; her health is very poor, her language is likened to a drunken sailor, she looks at least twenty years older than her real age, and she is living a sinful life. The difference, I believe, is the forgiveness factor. You can't even mention this guy's name around our friend without her going into all kinds of angry language and hurtful statements about him and his wife. She gets upset, her face gets red, and you can see the anger seething just under the surface. The names she calls this guy are pretty horrific, and it becomes obvious that whatever peace she thought she had made was, indeed, not made at all. Forgiveness, it's a healer!

Our friend has since passed away and gone to be with the Lord. My husband and I were with her on her deathbed, and we strongly urged her to finally, once and for all, forgive the man she was unable to forgive. Praise the Lord! She did forgive him at the last hour. My husband and I saw the release and the forgiveness wash over her face, and we saw the peace of God flood her. She died peaceably, and we know she went straight into the loving, merciful arms of Jesus. She is waiting for us in heaven, and we can't wait to be reunited with her.

———————————

I have seen the effects of nonforgiveness and they are ugly. It is painful to look at. People who refuse to forgive walk around with dour and sad faces, irritation boiling over to rudeness; they are impatient people who simply don't have the time of day for anyone or anything. The anger, bitterness, rage, and ultimately hate, eats them away on the inside. It is much easier to hand that unforgiveness over to God and allow Him to deal with it and the person who caused such turmoil and pain. The sad fact of the matter is that we want that control. We want to get back and get even with that person. We want to bring about justice and our own righteousness. Friend, listen to one who speaks from experience: God can do far worse things to that person who wounded you than the best plan you could ever come up with. I have an example for that as well.

Like I have told you, my mother and father refuse to repent or acknowledge their sin before God. They are ignoring Him hoping that He will just leave them alone. What they don't realize is that they have a daughter who loves them very much and wants the family reconciled and healed as a whole and not just one or two parts healed. So I have been praying literally for years for reconciliation of my family. I don't know if I will ever see this in my lifetime here on earth, but I have a hope and a faith in God so strong that I know He can do miracles even today.

God told me through prayer and Scripture that He loves me and He wanted me to be removed from my family and to stop trying to reconcile the family by myself. I had sent letter upon letter to my mother in an attempt to get her to see the truth of her actions. God hardened her heart toward me and she never saw the true meaning of my letters, nor did she feel or see my love and forgiveness for her and my father. It felt like I was talking to a brick wall. I could not get through to her.

Once God had me out of that picture, He told me He was going to bring calamity on my parents and He would escalate as necessary to get their attention. I prayed for mercy for them and prayed that He would not unleash His full anger and wrath upon them. I sent my mother another letter attempting to warn her of God's anger and wrath against them. I gave them the woes that God gave me and quoted Scripture. I begged her to listen; I begged her to repent and acknowledge her sin before God. She wouldn't listen to me.

I started hearing about problems they were facing. My mother was diagnosed with diabetes. My father fell and hurt his shoulder pretty bad; then he was involved in a pretty serious traffic accident that totaled his car. My brother was arrested for domestic violence. My father developed shingles. My mother was admitted to the hospital with heart issues.

As I heard of these problems, I sent my mother yet another letter and told her that God was trying to get their attention and they were not listening. I, again, repeated the woes God had given me and quoted Scripture in an attempt to open her eyes. She sent me a letter stating she was busy in some club or society organization and that she simply didn't have time to answer my letter, but that she would get around to it. Once again, my attempt to get them to take responsibility for their sin had fallen on deaf ears. What will it take? What will God have to do to get their attention? I really don't want to know, because when they are hurting, I am hurting too.

Do you see how God takes control of the situation and works on people? Yes, He does discipline His children. My mother is not listening. My father is not listening. They are ignoring God and that is not a good situation to be in. God has afflicted my parents and has done far worse to them in an attempt to get their attention than any plan I could have dreamed up to get them back for the wounds they have caused me.

Now, I need to tell you something that you need to be very careful of here. When I forgave my parents, it was not so God could step in and skewer them. I didn't step out of the way and ask God to hurt them worse than I was capable of doing. Forgiveness is truly releasing the person who wounded you into God's hands and allowing God to work on their heart. Forgiveness is not handing someone over to God and asking Him to take revenge for you. You must forgive the person from your heart and let him or her go. Don't wish him or her any ill or harm.

This is a good definition of forgiveness: There was a woman who was violated and brutally raped one night. She was an innocent victim, a beautiful girl and only twenty-five. The man was never convicted and was allowed to walk the streets. This woman went on with her life, went to counseling, found Jesus, and accepted Him as her Savior. Jesus spoke to her through the radio, maybe a Bible study, and a few sermons and was prompting her to forgive the man who raped her. Through many tears and prayer, she was finally able to forgive this man. The woman later found out that this man ended up inheriting a lot of money and lived high on the hog the rest of his days. The woman trusted God and believed Jesus when He told her that "Vengeance is Mine says the Lord." He will repay the evil that was done to her; He will see that justice is done. So she decided not to be bitter or angry with the man she had truly forgiven. That is an example of true forgiveness.

Did your anger rise up? Maybe you just got angry with me. How could she say such a thing? Could you forgive that guy? It would be pretty difficult. How dare I suggest that the woman forgive such a vile thing that was done to her? She has a right to hate that man! True enough, and I agree with you. She has every right to hate this guy and want all kinds of bad things done to him. She would be right if she were to take her own revenge against him. But these are things that the world says are okay and not what Jesus says are okay.

> But I tell you who hear me: Love your enemies, do good to those who hate you, bless those who curse you, pray for those who mistreat you. If someone strikes you on one cheek, turn to him the other also. If someone takes your cloak, do not stop him from taking your tunic.
>
> Luke 6:27–30

Pretty hard words to read, hear, and comprehend, aren't they? I am not the one who is telling you to forgive that person who wounded you; Jesus is. Let Him have that person and let Him deal with them in His time and according to His justice and authority. When you can do that, you are free indeed!

I want you to know that I don't say these words lightly or glibly. Beloved, I have been there. I have been violated, abused, deserted, abandoned, betrayed, and shunned and I know how it feels to want that sweet revenge. But that is not the way of God and that is not how He expects us to behave and conduct ourselves. We are called to a higher calling. He expects more from us because we are children of the King. We, all who have accepted Jesus as our Lord and Savior, are heirs to the thrown of God! That is huge!

Because we have such a high calling and are children of the Most High King, He calls us to a higher standard than the world. He also blesses and shows favor to His children who obey Him. He knows it is not easy to forgive someone who wounded you to the very core. He knows that full well. Jesus, God's only begotten Son, was tortured and died a very painful death for you and for me. He had done nothing wrong! He was sinless. He was the only one who walked on this earth without sin and without the sin nature you and I carry around with us on a daily basis.

Do you remember what Jesus said on the cross when He was dying? You have to first remember what happened to Him. He was mocked, slandered, gossiped about, made fun of, humiliated, spit on, beaten, tortured, whipped, and flogged to the point where His back was literally ripped open and the bone of His spine was exposed. He was nailed to a wooden cross with metal spikes driven into his hands and feet and left to die the very painful, agonizing death of suffocation. If anyone had a right to hate and want revenge, it was Jesus.

So what did Jesus do and say with all His authority and power and might and strength? He could have called legions of angels to come to His defense and rescue; He could have spoken one word and destroyed all of the people who had brutalized him; He could have squashed them like ants. What did He do?

In Luke 23:34: Jesus said, "Father, forgive them, for they do not know what they are doing." And they divided up his clothes by casting lots. Whoa! Are you kidding me? He forgave them? After all the abuse and torture and pain they had put Him through? Yes. He forgave them. Why? "Because they do not know what they are doing."

Are you telling me that the guy who raped that beautiful twenty-five-year-old woman and possibly screwed up her life didn't know what he was doing? I would imagine that guy knew what he was doing, just like the men torturing Jesus knew what they were doing, but they really didn't understand or know what they were doing. They are listening to the suggestions of satan and his demons. They are lost and without Christ. They have justified their actions in their own hearts and minds and do not know the mind of Christ. No, they do not know what they are doing. Please hear me on this.

The behavior of the people who tortured and crucified Jesus, the man who raped that woman, your abuser, and my abuser were not justified in the eyes of God. There will be consequences for their actions and they will have to answer for what they have done. They do not get away scot-free. There will be justice. Just because you can't see the justice doesn't mean that God won't judge them. When you trust God with your abuse, it is called faith.

My friend, I know you are hurting. I can feel your pain as I type this. God brought many images to my mind, and the tears haven't stopped flowing yet. You have gone through so much. I'm so sorry. Give it to God and let Him heal you. Stop drinking the poison you intended for the person who hurt you. You are the one who will die and suffer. Let it go.

When you can trust God enough with the person who wounded you, you are truly free. The past has no claim on you and you are no longer living under the law, but rather under grace. Grace is a much better way to live your life. There is so much freedom, peace, and love. I wish I could share the feeling with you. The closest thing I can compare this feeling to is riding a black stallion bareback with your hair streaming out behind you flying down the beach or a wooded path with not a care in the world: freedom. People have killed for it; people have died for it; all you have to do is forgive and you will be flooded with it!

Let's review the facts:

1. How many times does Jesus tell us to forgive? Seventy-seven times. As long as there are sinners and imperfect people on this earth, we will have to continually forgive those who wound us. Sometimes those wounds

are small and sometimes those wounds are big and contain lifelong pain. You will heal. Jesus loves you and does not want to see you hurt. He will heal you if you allow Him to.

2. Benefits to forgiveness include favor and blessing from God, a knowledge that God will forgive us as we have forgiven others, and freedom from anger, bitterness, and revenge. Stevie Ray Vaughn has a song with a lyric that goes like this, "I was looking for revenge; thank God it never found me." Keep this in mind; there is a lot of truth to be said about that.

3. The hard truth is that if Jesus can forgive the men who brutalized Him, then you can forgive the person who wounded you. If you say that you can't, then you are calling God a liar and saying that Jesus's death on the cross meant nothing. You are also saying that you are above God and can judge better than Him. Not a good place to be. It is not easy. Believe me. It is not easy to forgive someone who wounded you to the core. But it is necessary to live the kind of free life God has called us to. For your own sake, please, I beg you, forgive. Let it go; give them up right now. In fact, let's go to prayer.

Father God, You are so powerful and mighty. We thank You for the gift of your Son, Jesus Christ. Thank You, Jesus, for bearing my stripes and dying my death that I deserved. Father, there is someone in our life right now (go ahead and name the person God has placed on your heart to forgive) and we are having a very hard time forgiving him/her. Oh, Father, he/she hurt us so deeply. You see the wounds deep within our spirit and soul. The pain is great, and our hearts are absolutely shattered. Father, we want revenge on this person for what they did to us, but we know that is not Your way. You have called us to forgive those who wound us, but sometimes, Father, those wounds are very deep and are almost too much to bear. Forgive us, Father, for wanting revenge and for wanting to hurt the person who hurt

us. Help us to forgive day by day and step by step. This isn't easy
for us, Lord, but we are willing to trust in You and have faith in
Your justice and Your authority. We ask that justice be done by
Your will and in Your time. We ask this in the name of our Lord
and Savior, Jesus Christ. Amen.

Questions to Ponder

1. How did you do in this chapter? I have to admit it was
   hard to write and it was even harder to read it back.
   Pretty tough stuff when you have a shattered heart.
   Did you make it through okay? I hope you didn't give
   up. You have come so far, and I am praying for you and
   asking God to give you the strength to finish this book
   and truly forgive those who have wounded you.

   _____

   _____

   _____

   _____

2. Take a look at the events leading up to Jesus's death on the cross. Take a minute and read the book of John. Pretty painful to look at. Can you identify with any of the pain that He went through? The humiliation, the agony, the knowledge that the people you love the most in the whole word have deserted you, hate you, and want to see your death. Does any of that sound familiar to you? What did Jesus say? Do you remember? Forgiven them, Father, for they know not what they are doing. Can you do this?

_____

_____

_____

_____

Accountability and Responsibility Versus Judgment

If your brother sins against you, go and show him his fault, just between the two of you. If he listens to you, you have won him over. But if he will not listen, take one or two others along, so that "every matter may be established by the testimony of two or three witnesses." If he refuses to listen to them, tell it to the church; and if he refuses to listen even to the church, treat him as you would a pagan or a tax collector.

Matthew 18:15–17

There is a very scary movement happening in this country. It seems that people are taking the judgment of people and their sin way out of context from the way that God had originally ordained it. We are not supposed to judge people, for in the way we judge people, that is how our heavenly Father will judge us. However, this is not a license to do whatever we want and think we do not have to be held accountable for our thoughts, words, and deeds.

My mother has done horrific damage to both my husband and me with her gossip, lies, and slandering. We have totally forgiven her; however, we have tried to hold her accountable for that sin. My mother has sent me many letters stating that I am not to judge her.

This has been taken out of context. God tells us not to judge others; however, as far as sin is concerned, you are to hold that person accountable and responsible. This has nothing to do with forgiving that person. Absolutely we are to forgive people for the sin they commit against us. It has everything to do with helping that person see the errors of his or her ways, and, as gently as you can through love, guide them back to God's word and *His* truth—not your truth or agenda.

If what my mother says is true and we are not to judge people for the sin they commit, then the same would hold true of people who rape, murder, steal, lie, and break the laws of society. Right? It stands to reason that if we are not to judge people for their actions, then we would be guilty of judging those who commit atrocities against others. Judging people and holding people accountable for their actions are two very distinct and separate issues. When someone breaks the law, he or she is punished justly and brought before (hopefully) an unbiased and fair judge to determine whether he or she is guilty of committing the crime he or she has been accused of.

Deuteronomy 27:19 says, "Cursed is the man who withholds justice from the alien, the fatherless or the widow." God has placed boundaries and put laws into place to govern a people in an attempt to keep sin at bay and uphold some semblance of righteousness. To say that we are never to judge anyone for anything is sin and is not of God.

God is the author and creator of justice. He allows us to judge fairly the sins of others. He expects us to hold one another accountable for the sin we see. However, we have to be very careful not to point out a sin in someone's life without first examining closely our own lives. If you accuse your neighbor of poor language and taking the Lord's name in vain, then you yourself have to examine your life and see if you do the same thing. That is what Jesus meant when he said in Matthew 7:3: "Why do you look at the speck of sawdust in your brother's eye and pay no attention to the plank in your own eye?"

Unfortunately, that is exactly what my mother has accused me of doing. The problem with that is I am not judging her; I am holding her accountable and responsible for the sin and damage she has poured out upon us. My husband and I do not gossip about other people. We do not spread rumors or hurtful words to harm others. One of the lies that my mother has spread around the family and to my husband's boss was that he was an alcoholic and he beat me. Now, that was a bald-faced lie and my mother knows it. She has no basis for this lie; she has no facts or proof to back up her claims. She started spreading this lie in an attempt to discredit and harm my husband in an attempt to hurt and get to me. God has called us to hold her accountable and responsible for spreading this lie throughout the family and to others. She has accused us of judging her.

Remember what Jesus said: If your brother (or someone) sins against you, talk with that person in private; don't embarrass them in front of others. You are instructed to show them the error of their ways, just the two of you. If that doesn't work, then you are to call in two or three witnesses and, again, try to get the person to see their sin. If that doesn't work, then you are to go before the church and try to resolve it that way. Finally, if that doesn't work, then you are to treat them as pagans and tax collectors. In other words, have nothing to do with them!

I went to my mother and had a five-hour conversation with her. I shared my pain with her and she betrayed me. She brought over my grandmother one day in October and had her own agenda, but my husband was there and before three witnesses, we again tried to share our pain with her and tried to show her what she had done to us. She got up and left and started spreading more lies. We tried to go to the church, our pastor, and talk with him, but that didn't result in any real results. So we did exactly as the Lord had commanded us to do and have stayed away from her. The Lord told us to back off; we have done all we could, and now it was His turn to try to reach her through other means.

The whole point of this chapter is that when you hold someone accountable for his or her sin, you are allowing God to come in and change their heart. Only God can open the eyes of the sinful and lead them to repentance. Sometimes He uses other people to get the ball rolling. He sends in messengers to reach the person who sinned against you. The reaction or response that person displays when confronted with the truth is not your issue or problem.

In the case of my mother, she refuses to listen and desperately wants to sweep everything under the rug and have a wonderful relationship. This is not realistic thinking, because there is no change or accountability taken on her part. That is not my issue or my problem. I have to leave her response in God's hands no matter how much it hurts or how irritated I get. I am simply the messenger, not the judge and jury.

In this example, I will show you the difference between judging others and holding them accountable for their actions. There was a man who robbed a bank at gunpoint and walked away with $100,000. The man was caught and brought to trial before a judge. Now, if we are not to judge others for their wrongdoing, then the judge in this case would probably say something like this, "Son, what you have done is not good. You scared a lot of people, causing trauma, and the people feared for their very lives. You took what did not belong to you. In fact, you took money that people worked hard for and were saving to live on in their later years. But since we are not to judge others, I will let you go and ask that you please not do that again."

Now, I know that is absolutely ridiculous. I want you to see the extent of the liberalness that this country is going toward in an attempt to have no accountability for anything that people do or say.

When you hold someone accountable for his or her wrongdoing, the same scenario above would go something like this with the judge saying, "Son, what you have done is horrific. You terrified people and made them fear for their very lives. You stole money that did not belong to you, and you didn't even think about the people you were stealing from. You have committed a very grievous act, and I am going to find you guilty of your actions. Because I do not want you to do this to anyone else, I am holding you accountable for what you have done and you will pay a very high price for the lives you have terrorized. You will be remanded to prison for twenty years without parole. Case closed."

See the difference? Holding people accountable for the sin they have done to you or to others is far different than judging them. By the way, sin is sin is sin is sin. God views all sin the same. We are the ones who place degrees of importance on sin. We say that rape is worse than lying or that murder is worse than gossiping, but God sees all sin the same—unacceptable to a pure and holy God. The punishment for sin is the same whether you lie or steal or murder or gossip or even over eat. The punishment of sin is death. Sin is sin is sin. The Bible tells us if we are guilty of breaking one law, then we are guilty of breaking all the laws. Hard stuff to swallow, but those are not my words; they are God's words.

We are called to forgive those who sin against us. We are also called to hold accountable and responsible those who do wrong in the sight of the Lord. We are not to play God and judge people unjustly or to help further our agenda. This is a very fine line, and people can be so easily led astray and go from one extreme to another. God is the ultimate judge. He will judge the living and the dead and all the inhabitants of the earth both above and below. However, He has placed in us His trust to point out deliberate sin in one another's lives.

I have to be so very careful here. This subject is so touchy, because people are clamoring not to be judged but to live as they want to. This is really not what God had in mind. My personal opinion is that God has called us to hold one another accountable so that change can come and turn the person in the right direction as a bit in a horse's mouth turns the horse. I truly believe that God did not want our own agendas to cloud over the truth of His Word.

The best example I can give you of this would be to go back to my family situation. My mother claims I am judging her. No. I am holding her accountable and responsible for the damage she has caused to both my husband and I. To ignore that damage, sweep it under the rug, or hold her harmless of her actions is not helping her to change. In actuality, it is enabling her to stay in her sin.

God does not want you to keep on sinning, and there are consequences for sin, especially for deliberate sin. In the case of my mother, if I did not hold her accountable for the damage she had done, she would not be receptive to change. Because I have held her accountable, I have taken away her perch and stand on which she says, "I have done nothing wrong. My actions and words are justified in my own mind." That is a lie, and I will not allow her to live that lie knowing what I know about God and His wrath against deliberate sin.

———————

Let's go back to the guy who robbed the bank at gunpoint. Do you think this guy would have stopped robbing banks if the judge had simply scolded him and allowed him back on the streets? I doubt it. Change comes as a result of being held accountable for wrongdoing and wrong behavior. Change also comes as we experience the consequences of our sin.

———————

I want this to be heard loud and clear. I love my mother. If I didn't love her, I would not hold her accountable. In fact, when you get right down to it, if you have someone to hold you accountable for your actions and deeds, you will be blessed and less likely to go astray. If you refuse to be held accountable for anything, then you are only deceiving yourself and the truth is not in you. These are hard words to hear, but they are the absolute truth. When you refuse to be held accountable, you are saying that, in effect, you don't need God and you are perfectly capable of choosing between right and wrong at all times. This is a lie. The heart, in its very nature, is deceitful and will always lead you astray unless you are grounded in the following:

1. God, Jesus as your personal Lord and Savior

2. The very Word of God, the Bible, breathed into words, and

3. Someone you can totally trust who loves you and has your best interests at heart to hold you accountable for your actions and deeds.

My husband is my best friend and does a great job of holding me accountable. He will honestly tell me in love and truth when I have said or done something that was not right or that was maybe hurtful to another person. I also have a very dear friend and sister in Christ who holds me accountable. I love these people more than life itself, but not more than my God and Savior, Jesus Christ. I love them because they are honest enough and bold enough to say, "Hey, um, Marie, you know I love you and I wouldn't tell you this if I didn't have to, but what you said or did back there was not nice, and God probably wasn't pleased." Do I always agree with these two dear people? No! In fact, more times than not, I probably grumble some reply and then the Holy Spirit comes in and lets me know that what they have said is right and I better heed that information and repent. Down on my knees I go!

That is another way for you to distinguish between being judged and being held accountable. If someone confronts you and you know what he or she is saying is true, the Holy Spirit will convict you; this is accountability. Judging others is making assumptions or accusations of a person with surface knowledge. An example of this would be judging someone who attends church in a pair of jeans and a stained sweatshirt or judging someone who has committed a crime against society and continuing on that punishment by not working with that person or treating him or her harshly when you are in a position of authority. This is judging that person when you are not the judge.

Please hear my heart. It is so very hard to hear when we have sinned in any aspect of our lives, regardless of whether that sin is in wrong decisions when raising our children, gossiping about another person, listening to gossip and chiming in, or committing any kind of deliberate wrong action. We don't want to believe we are wrong or have sinned. We want so badly to think that we are good and our actions, thoughts, and words are right and everyone who tries to correct us is wrong. We want to believe that we know more and our decisions are right to us and right before God. It is hard to hear when we mess up. No one likes to be wrong and no one likes to be told he or she is wrong.

When we can come to the realization that we have hurt others, we have made wrong decisions, and that we have sinned against Almighty God, then we put ourselves in a position for change and God can help us. He can hold us and tell us that He loves us and while He does not condone what we have done, He graciously forgives us and will show us how to handle the situation better next time. What He gives you is mercy and grace. Left unchecked, ignoring accountability leads us into more sin and farther away from God. Remember, you can never go anywhere that God is not, but—and this is a big but—there are always consequences for sin. Always. God loves you, yes; He will forgive you, but you will have to pay whatever consequences there are for that sin.

I would like to give you an example of consequences for sin. David, another hero of mine in the Bible, totally blew it one evening. His men were in battle and he was walking the rooftop of his palace. Why he was walking around is unclear. The Bible just says that he was in bed sleeping and then he decided to get up and walk around on his roof. Maybe he wanted to clear his head or maybe he just needed some fresh air. Whatever the reason, he was walking around on the roof and he happened to gaze out over the rooftops and happened to see a very beautiful woman taking a bath.

Now, that is kind of interesting. I, for one, would never take a bath on the rooftop, but apparently, in those days, it was acceptable to have the bathtub on the roof of your home. Well, David fell into lust—big time! He absolutely had to have that woman no matter the cost. The woman, whose name was Bathsheba, was married to Uriah the Hittite. Uriah had gone to battle with the other men.

Long story short, David slept with Bathsheba and she became pregnant. David eventually had Uriah killed by deliberately putting him on the front lines of the battle. Eventually, David was confronted by Nathan, and David repented to the Lord for his sin of adultery and murder. However, and here is the point, there was a consequence to be paid. David and Bathsheba lost the son they had conceived in adultery. There are always consequences for your sin. You can read the whole account of David and Bathsheba in 2 Samuel chapters eleven and twelve.

━━━━━━━━━━━━━━━

Before I go on to my next example, I want to tell you that when you have sinned and you have been held accountable and you take responsibility for what you have done, God will test you in the very thing you messed up in. For example, I used to have a huge problem with exaggeration. I would put my own spin on the truth to make myself look important. God finally got my attention and showed me that I do this. After I had repented and asked God for help, He would place me deliberately in situations where I would have the opportunity to either exaggerate again or stick to the truth. Sometimes, I would fail and the Holy Spirit was right there to convict me and I knew I had messed up again. A few times of having to go back and say, "Uh, listen, what I said back there, that wasn't really the truth. I exaggerated this part," really makes you conscious and you are less likely to repeat the sin.

If you have to go back and make your wrongs right, you will think twice about making that same mistake again. I have a great example of this. When I was about seven years old, my mother took my grandmother, brother, and me shopping. We went into a store and I wanted a piece of candy. My mother said I could not have a piece of candy and off we went. Well, I was determined to have that piece of candy and stole it from the store. I was not thinking clearly when I started unwrapping the candy in front of my mother. To her credit, she made me go back to the store and return the candy and apologize to the clerk for taking it. That was the hardest thing in the world for me to do, but do you know to this day, I have not stolen so much as a pen or pencil from anyone? Of course, the true repercussions of this act came down hard upon me when my mother got me home. I probably deserved some sort of punishment; even though returning the candy was punishment enough and I had learned a very valuable lesson about stealing something that is not yours.

When you refuse to be held accountable for your actions, it is easy to continue to commit the same sin over and over again. Had my mother not made me take the candy back and apologize to the clerk, I probably would still be stealing to this day! I would invite you to test this theory. If you lie or exaggerate—or maybe you are prone to gossiping—whatever you continue to do over and over again that you know is wrong, take it to God. Repent and ask for help in changing. If you have to go back to someone and tell that person that you gossiped about him or her or lied or exaggerated the truth, you will be more conscious the next time you have an opportunity to sin in that way again. You will think twice, and you will remember the embarrassment and pain of having to admit you sinned and did wrong. It serves as a great teacher in life!

─────────────────

King David asked the Lord where he could go from God's eyes. He said if he were to go up to heaven that God would be there; that if we went to the depths of the earth that God would be there also. We cannot escape from God and He knows everything!

I am reminded of two people who tried to hide from God but failed miserably.

> Then the man and his wife heard the sound of the LORD God as he was walking in the garden in the cool of the day, and they hid from the LORD God among the trees of the garden.
>
> Genesis 3:8

Adam and Eve could not hide from God and neither can we when we sin against Him or others. He will eventually find us and hold us accountable. As for me, I would rather be held accountable here on this earth than wait and get before Almighty God and have to answer for what I have done face-to-face. I would rather rejoice when I see my Lord rather than cringe because of some sin I had not repented of or refused to be held accountable for on this earth.

This was a hard chapter to write, because, like you, I have to take a look at some of the sin in my life as well. Remember, I am not perfect and neither are you. We all sin, but the point is that we can turn from that sin with the help of others pointing it out to us, going back and making the wrongs we have done right, and allowing God to change us from the inside out.

I would invite you right now to take a look at your life. Has someone in your life been trying to hold you accountable for something you might have said or done to another person? Have you tried to say that they are judging you? You know what you have done; the Holy Spirit will convict you of all wrongdoing and lead you into the truth if you will let Him. If you refuse, then God has to use some other way to get your attention and bring you back to the original sin you committed. This could take a while. Remember the story of King David and Bathsheba? It took King David one full year to acknowledge his sin with Bathsheba and take responsibility for his actions. Talk about not wanting to be held accountable!

King David was confronted by Nathan the Prophet. Nathan got in David's face! Now King David could have had this prophet killed, but deep down David knew that Nathan was right, but he didn't come to repentance for a full year! David knew what he had done. He knew he had committed adultery with Bathsheba and knowingly and purposefully had her husband killed in battle. Adultery and murder are both grievous sins against the Lord. Nathan the Prophet tried to hold David accountable, but he would have none of it. God had to take drastic measures to get David's attention and He eventually repented and God was able to change his ways and He did forgive David. David couldn't sweep his sin under the rug and pretend it never happened. He couldn't go on believing that everything was okay and we can all be one big happy family. Nope. Accountability—it is a good thing.

If you don't have someone right now that will hold you accountable, then find a friend or pastor, someone you can trust completely, to point out your sin. You will never regret it and you will find favor with the Lord. It takes a very mature and humble person to admit when he or she is wrong. It is the first step to growth and freedom. When you admit you are wrong, you take another piece of yourself away from satan. The rat, as I am often heard referring to him as, is all about pride, and when you puff yourself up with pride and can't admit when you mess up, then satan has you right where he wants you and that is not following God but following him.

Let's review the facts:

1. When someone holds you accountable for sin in your life, he or she is not judging you. If someone speaks to you in truth and love and points out something you have done to him or her or someone else, this is love. If someone judges you for your appearance or continues to treat you with harshness after you have admitted your sin, this can be classified as judgment. Part of being held accountable for your sin is experiencing the consequences and, in as much as it is up to you, making the wrong right.

2. If you refuse to be held accountable for something you know you have done wrong, then you will reap worse consequences and God will pursue you and keep throwing that sin in your face until you repent and agree to be held responsible and accountable for your thoughts, words, or deeds. The Holy Spirit's conviction will be powerful and very strong within you. He will lead you into all truth.

3. God disciplines His children and those He loves. If you are open to being held accountable, you will find favor in God's eyes and He will help you change and grow in Him.

Questions to Ponder

1. Do you have someone in your life who holds you accountable? Do you resist being held accountable? Do you constantly deny the same accusation over and over, even though you know it is the truth?

_____

_____

_____

_____

2. Are you mature enough to honestly, through love and truth, hold someone you care about accountable? Can you point out the sin in someone else's life using love instead of strife? If you can't, then you are not the right person to hold him or her accountable. Give it to someone else to do. It may be that you are too close to the situation.

_____

_____

_____

_____

3. Are you okay with leaving the responses and results up to God after you have confronted someone in his or her sin either against you or against someone else? His or her response is not your issue. That is between that person and God. If he or she gets angry with you, he or she is really getting angry with him or herself first and then with God for not allowing him or her to get away with whatever it is that he or she has done wrong.

_____

_____

_____

_____

I would like to pray for you, as this was a hard chapter to digest.

Father God, we all want so desperately to look good in Your eyes. We want to cover our sins and sweep them under the rug rather than allow You or others You place in our lives to hold us accountable for that sin. Father, please forgive us. Please open our eyes to Your truth and help us to first see the sin in our lives and then to change and become more like your Son, Jesus Christ. We are blind to our own sin, Father, and I would ask that You would come into our lives in a very powerful way and help us to first get right with You and then help us to make the wrongs we have done right. I pray that You would have mercy on us and gently lead us into Your truth and Your way for our lives. I ask this in Jesus's name alone. Amen."

Can You Love Your Enemies?

> But I tell you who hear me: Love your enemies, do good to those who hate you, bless those who curse you, pray for those who mistreat you.
>
> Luke 6:27–28

Hate and anger, it's all the rage! In this world, it is so easy, if not fun, to hate those who have hurt us. To hate those who hurt us or wounded us is definitely in style. But that is not God's way. God expects so much more of us. If you are a follower of Jesus, then you must know that He said to love your enemies and pray for those who mistreat you. Those are pretty hard words to swallow. After all, when we have been wounded by someone or deeply hurt, our first response is to get back, make that person feel the pain he or she has caused us. But if we look closely at Scripture, we learn that it is God's job to bring about justice and pay back evil, not ours.

Romans 12:19 says, "Do not take revenge, my friends, but leave room for God's wrath, for it is written, 'It is mine to avenge; I will repay,' says the Lord." When we make a decision to get back at someone for hurting us, we are assuming God's role and we are basically telling God that we can handle justice better than He can. Quite frankly, I don't want God's job; it is too hard.

After the painful memories of my childhood had unblocked, my mother's betrayal of my innermost secret confessions and the continued gossip and lies she spread, I was pretty angry, not to mention my heart was shattered. I wanted to strike back hard, fast, and furious. Did you know that satan loves to help people take revenge? Unfortunately, satan comes up with the best revenge plans of anyone, but they only bring further heartache and pain. You think you will be justified if you retaliate and hurt the person who wounded you, but it will only bring you more pain and anguish. Oh, it may feel good for a time, but then guilt and shame will set in and you will not feel any better about taking revenge than you did when you were first wounded.

I wanted revenge. I wanted my mother to hurt and feel as much pain as she caused me. I wanted her to feel the heat from embarrassment and the guilt and shame of her gossiping and slander. I had a great idea of going to the prosecuting attorney in our town and bringing up charges of slander and defamation of character against my mother. In addition, I was going to get a gag order against her, forbidding her from spreading more lies, gossip, and slander about us. I was almost ready to go through with my plan when God tapped me on the shoulder and gently told me that what I was planning was revenge.

I argued with Him and said, "No, Lord. This is not revenge. This is self-preservation! This is protecting myself and my husband from any more gossip and lies."

The Lord spoke to my heart and said, "Self-protection is a sin and will place a wall between you and others in an effort to protect yourself from getting emotionally hurt. Just because you get a piece of paper telling your mother not to gossip and spread lies does not mean she will stop." Oh. He had me there. Short of my mother dying, I did not have a foolproof way of silencing her. The Lord then told me that He knew about the gossip and lies that my mother was spreading and He had a plan to help her see the error of her ways. I didn't want her to see the error of her ways; I wanted her to ingest the poison she had spewed forth from her lips!

Then God started speaking to me through the book of Proverbs.

A gossip betrays a confidence; so avoid a man who talks too much.

> Proverbs 20:19

A perverse man stirs up dissension, and a gossip separates close friends.

> Proverbs 16:28

What God was showing me was that I did not have to do anything to achieve retaliation against my mother. She would self-destruct all on her own and people would eventually find out that she had lied. God wanted me to live the life He called me to and never mind about taking revenge.

―――――――――

Okay, so what does all this have to do with loving your enemies? Well, my mother had singlehandedly turned most of our family, our church family, and my husband's bosses against us through her manipulation, lies, gossip, and slander. One of my fervent prayers was that our family would be reconciled and the truth would come out. Proverbs 17:9 says, "He who covers over an offense promotes love, but whoever repeats the matter separates close friends." The message was clear. To attack my mother legally and bring shame upon her through the public eye was just a continuation of her anger and the sin that had affected this family going back four generations. When I started to pray for my mother, God showed me that He loves her too. She has listened to the wrong voice and only God could bring her back to the path of righteousness and He didn't need any help from me, thank you very much!

―――――――――

My mother is a very prideful person. She has to look good at all times in front of everyone. Proverbs 16:5 says, "The Lord detests all the proud of heart. Be sure of this: They will not go unpunished." So there it was. God knew exactly what my mother had been doing and it had not escaped His eyes. He knew that the lies and gossip she was spreading around were only an attempt to make herself look good in the eyes of men, so she did not have to explain the truth of why her daughter wanted nothing to do with her. She had to make up lies about her daughter and son-in-law to save face with family and friends. She had to look like the victim in this situation and, in some form, she is the victim, but she also knows right from wrong. God assured me that she would not go unpunished for these evil, wicked acts.

When you know God has seen your heart and knows the truth that surrounds your pain, rest assured He will see to it those responsible for your pain will not go unpunished. Please hear me on this: God is the one to repay evil, not you and not me. Jesus calls us to love our enemies. It's a tall order with tall blessings. Just as God disciplines those He loves and guides them back to the path of righteousness, He also rewards those who obey Him and His commands.

When you love your enemies, you take on the very character of God. He loves everyone. See if you can get your mind around this. God loves Marilyn Manson, a self-professed follower of satan, as much as He loves you and me. That is very hard to wrap our minds around. When we understand that God created all of us and He is our heavenly Father, it makes it easier to understand His love for His wayward children. However, we all have a choice to make and the choice we make will bring consequences or rewards.

I assume some of you reading this have children. Let's take your child for an example and help you see what I mean here. I assume you love your child. If your child were to rob a bank and kill the teller, would you love that child less than when your child was born? I am sure you would not be very happy with that child, and you may even chastise him or her, and you would probably become quite angry with that child, but the question is, would you love that child less than when he or she was born? My guess is no.

Now, this is how the Almighty Father loves your child. Father God created this child in his or her mother's womb. His love for that child, no matter what the child chooses in this life, cannot falter or be removed. God loves His creation and His children. He may get angry with His children; He may discipline them, but He will always love them. God will even allow that child to choose hell for all eternity, but the love of God will never be less for that child, regardless of the path they choose. Of course, God would have all His children choose His son, Jesus Christ, as their personal Lord and Savior, so we can all be in heaven with Him. God gave us free-will and it is a choice and the choice is ours to make. God will never force Himself on anyone. He would never hold a gun to your head and say, "Choose Me or die." No, we make the choice to live with Him forever or to be separated from Him forever and live in hell.

And so He calls us to love our enemies, which are His children. Those of us who love the Lord our God with all our hearts, minds, strength, and soul know His mighty love for us. Let me give you another analogy on loving your enemies. If you have more than one child, then you know about sibling rivalry.

My brother and I used to fight all the time. I loved my brother, but I was constantly picking on him and lording my two whole years of seniority over him. When you see your children fighting and arguing, does that hurt you? Do you get angry when you see your children really going at it? How do you think God feels when one of His children deeply wounds another? God is the ultimate parent and He loves all of us, His children. When we wound one another, it hurts Him.

God calls us to love one another just as He first loved us. It is not a suggestion and God does not say, "If you feel like it." No. God commands us to love one another. I can hear someone right now: "You don't know what I went through! You don't know how my body, mind, and spirit were wounded." True enough, but God knows.

If you need an example of this, we have to take a look at Jesus's life again. He went through all the pain and hurt that we will ever experience, and yet, as He was dying on the cross for your sins and mine, He was calling out to the heavenly Father to forgive those who had crucified Him. Talk about loving your enemies! Not only did He love His enemies, but He prayed for them as well. He led the example we should follow when we have been horribly wounded by another person. Pray for them. When we pray, we open the door for God to work not only in our own lives but also in the lives of those who have wounded us.

Do you think you can change the person who wounded you by retaliation? If you strike back or try to hurt the person who hurt you, do you think that would bring that person closer to God or would it push him or her farther away on the dark path he or she is currently traveling on? Only God can change the hearts of people—not men, women, or children. No one can change your heart but God. Only God can change the mind and heart of the person who wounded you.

So how do we help God change that wicked person's heart? By praying for that person. God works through the open doors of our prayers. If we sincerely pray for the person who wounded us, then God can start working in that person's life. This is exactly what has been happening to my mother. I have been praying for her for several years now and God is just now starting to work in her life. It is not pretty. Lots of bad things are going on in her life right now that I am sure she doesn't like. I certainly don't wish her any ill or harm, but at the same time, I can see God's hand clearly in her life as He tries different ways of getting her attention. The horrible question of "What is it going to take?" keeps coming to my mind, and I really don't want to know.

Since I have been praying for my mother, God has shown me how to love her. Yes, you heard me right, actually love her. I can't do this on my own; God has to love her through me, but it is love nonetheless. In fact, I love her so much that I pray that God would have mercy on her and I actually pity her and feel sorry for her. I have to remind myself that she is a child of abuse too. Abuse begets abuse. Just like evil begets evil. If you show evil to someone, chances are you will get treated the same way. However, if someone shows evil to you and you repay him or her with kindness or love, that is of God.

━━━━━━━━━━━━━

As you can tell from reading this book so far, I love stories. I love reading stories, hearing stories, and telling stories. I love stories! I used to sit at my grandmother's feet and listen to her stories over and over again. I never grew tired of hearing her stories of the old country and her adventures growing up. You know, Jesus told stories too. That is how He got a lot of His messages across to people. If you are like me, you learn better through stories.

I am reminded of a story about repaying good for evil. There was a man who crept into a wealthy man's home one night and took some valuables. He stole silverware, plates, vases, and pretty much everything he could stuff into a bag. The thief was caught red pawed by the police. They had watched him creep into the man's home and knew he was stealing. The owner of the house came down a large staircase, and the officer, with the man captured by the scruff of the neck, asked the homeowner if he knew this man.

Now, the owner of the house was a godly man, and he knew this guy was stealing from him, but material possessions didn't mean that much to him. So he told the officer that he had authorized the man to come in and take what he needed, and then the owner of the house gave the thief two gold candlestick holders and told him that he forgot those and he knew that he needed them. Incredible! How many of us would have run to the closet for our shotgun or to the phone to call the police or let the guard dog out of the back room? My hand is raised! I would not have been that kind to a thief!

My point is that the reaction of the homeowner is exactly what Jesus would have required and expected of us. Jesus told us that if a man takes your tunic, give him your cloak also. Don't you know that whatever is stolen from you, God will repay you and then some? It is true. After the fear of someone breaking into my house had passed, I can really identify with the homeowner because material possessions simply don't mean that much to me. The fact that someone broke into my home is scary business, and that is probably what I would react to.

If everyone went around giving kindness for evil, what kind of world would we have? I think we would have a lot of broken hearts that would repent of their sin and turn from their wicked ways. I think satan would be defeated in his tracks as ruler of this world before the Lord sends him to hell for all eternity. What if we just started in our own world? When someone says an ugly word to you, smile and tell him that God loves him and that you will pray for him. Now for the serious physical damage that people can inflict upon you—rape, physical trauma—you need to go to the authorities and report them, so that these people are not allowed to hurt anyone else again.

———————————

In the case of my mother, I seriously thought about bringing child abuse charges against her, but the statute of limitations had run out. But what would that have solved? She is not going to have any more children, and she will never have access to any grandchildren. No, the only thing I can do is pray for her and allow God to show her the evil she has done in His sight. There is a fine line between knowing when to prosecute someone and when to let go. If she commits a grievous criminal act against anyone else, then, yes, she should be reported and criminal action should be taken.

I know I have to be careful here. There are people out there that go to both extremes: those who will prosecute anyone for any reason and those who won't prosecute people who need to be off the streets for fear of hurting others again. I am not talking about the extremes here. If you have been brutally violated and physically wounded and you have the capability of reporting that person to the authorities, then by all means, do just that. But if your wounds, like mine, happened when you were a child, and it is past history, I would not advise prosecuting the person who hurt you. God will deal with him or her in His time and in His way.

One thing I would caution you on is don't expect perfect justice from humans. It won't happen. Remember my story of the gal who was raped in a previous chapter? Her accuser basically got off scot-free and wasn't held to justice. God will judge those who hurt others. It may not be in your lifetime and you may never see true justice done, but rest assured God will handle that for you and all you need to do is trust Him.

Finally, when we start to pray for and eventually love our enemies, God can do some pretty amazing healing in our own hearts, minds, and spirits. This has happened for me. It wasn't until I forgave my mother and started praying for her that God really started healing me. He removed all of the hate, anger, rage, and other negative feelings I had toward my mother. Then He started showing me that my mother was repeating a sin cycle. He had me take a closer look into my past and see generational sin in action.

After I realized that my mother had been abused and this sin was cyclical, I was able to understand her a bit better. I did not condone her actions or her abuse, I simply understood it better. After the understanding and knowledge took hold, then God started prompting me to pray for her.

At first, I prayed that God would thump her. "Please God, infest her armpits with the fleas of a thousand camels!" He didn't like that and started directing my prayers toward her for understanding and truth to be poured into her like a drink offering. I didn't like that, so I tried to compromise by praying, "God, um, she hurt me really bad and has done some serious damage to both my husband and me. Could you please set her hair on fire but then put it out real quick?" He didn't like that either.

After wrestling with God on how to pray for my mother, He won out, and I ended up praying a prayer that went something like this: "Father God, You know the pain and hurt my mother has caused my husband and me. You have seen my wounds. You have placed Your healing love as salve on my wounds and they have started to heal. I wish no ill toward my mother and pray that You would bring about your justice with mercy, grace, and love. Break down the pride that exists within her and show her the error of her ways. Please forgive her, Father, as I have forgiven her, for she knows not what she has done, but she is living in total reaction to what she has learned and been taught by a sinful earthly father. I lift her to you, and ask it in Jesus's name. Amen." His reaction as I felt in my heart was, "Much better, child."

When we truly release someone who has wounded us into the Lord's hands, we are giving up our right to carry out justice as we see fit in our own eyes and allowing God to carry out His pure and holy justice that can actually change a heart for the better. We have to remember that God loves the one who wounded us as much as He loves us. That is very difficult for us to get our minds around. We don't want to think that a holy God could love the evil people of this world, but what we have to remember is that He causes the sun and rain to fall upon both the good and evil of this world.

What does that tell you? It tells me that He loves my mother as much as He loves me; however, He does not approve of her actions toward me and she will have to pay a price for that, either on this earth or when she meets Jesus face-to-face. If she waits until she meets Jesus face-to-face, it will be far worse for her because she will have nowhere to run or hide when He asks her the very difficult and painful questions of why she did what she did to the children He gifted her with. Yikes! If it were me, I would rather take my lumps here on earth rather than have to explain and give an account for unrepented sin in heaven.

My friend, I know this must be a very hard chapter for you to digest. It was hard to write this one. It is definitely not the way the world would have us treat such people who have wounded us. No, the world would have us go after that person tooth and nail and string him or her up for all his or her worth. That is not what God calls us to do. If you are a follower of Jesus, then you must love your enemies. I know that is hard to swallow and hard to get your mind around. If we are to survive and not drive ourselves crazy wishing horrible things on the person who wounded us, there is no other way.

I feel compelled to pray for you right now. I feel that someone who will read this book is really going to struggle with this part, and I would just like to pray for you because I can feel your pain in my heart and I know that what was done to you was not right, even in God's eyes.

> Father God, my heart bleeds for the person who is reading this part of the book right now. Chances are that this person has truly suffered evil at the hands of another person. You know that pain, Lord. You know that hurt, and You were in the midst of that abuse with him or her, just like You were with me in the midst of my suffering and abuse. Father, I would just ask that You strengthen the heart of this dear child of Yours right now. It is very difficult to love those who have wounded us so deeply, but that is what You call us to do. Give us Your strength, Your comfort, Your healing, and Your love right now. Wrap Your loving arms around my dear brother or sister reading this and simply hold him or her. Hold him or her, Father, as You have held me and shower them with Your love for You are no respecter of persons. Help him or her to pray for the one who wounded him or her.
>
> Father, it is not possible for us to love those who hurt us by ourselves. Through us, please love the person who wounded us and teach us how to love him or her as You love him or her. Help us to realize that the person who hurt us is Your child too, and You love him or her as You love us. We surrender the person who wounded us into Your mighty hands, our Father, and ask that you continue to guide us into Your truth and love for each other. In the precious loving name of Jesus, our Lord and Savior, I ask and pray. Amen.

My friend, my heart breaks for your pain. If you prayed this prayer with me, then I know that God held you up in His right hand and was holding you as you wept. I was crying too. Release your hate and anger once and for all and allow God to help you love your enemies. It won't be easy and you will have to work at it, but, in time, you will be able to pray for and eventually love your enemies. God can help you if you let Him.

Let's review the facts:

1. God commands us to love our enemies and to pray for them. We are incapable of doing this ourselves, so don't even try. You will fail every time. Through you, only God can love that person who wounded you so deeply. The question is will you let Him? I would welcome you to write down what you are feeling right now.

_____

_____

_____

_____

2. All the peoples of this earth were created by God. Much like sibling rivalry, when one person wounds another, it hurts God too. He doesn't like to see any of His children hurt or hurting or wounded or wounding others. He realizes that the people who hurt others are not listening to Him, but rather they are taking direct orders from satan.

3. My mind goes to the horrific atrocities committed by terrorists in our midst, so don't think I take lightly the wounds brought on by evil, wicked people. The point I am trying to make is that God is the only One who can change hearts. We do not condone the behavior or cruel actions of others, but we can pray for them and

place them in God's hands and allow Him to deal with their wickedness.

4. It is not easy to love our enemies or to even pray for them. In our human nature, we want to stomp on them and make them cry and hurt like they hurt us. If you belong to Jesus Christ, then you are set apart and are called to a higher calling. You must forgive those who hurt you and you must pray for them and ultimately come to love them. It is the way Jesus taught us. If we go around returning evil for evil, what has that gained us? More evil and more hurt and pain in the world. If we return good for evil, then we have planted a seed that God can grow and hopefully change the heart of the person who committed the evil in the first place.

Questions to Ponder

1. Can you love and pray for those who wounded you?

_____

_____

_____

_____

2. Is there someone in your life right now that you need to pray for? Someone who hurt you and wounded you deeply? You won't be able to do this on your own. You will need the power and truth of the Holy Spirit living within you to carry out this difficult task. The question then becomes, will you be available to God and allow Him to work through you to bring about that love for those who hurt you? If your answer is no, pray about it and see where God would take you.

_____

_____

_____

_____

3. So let's say you have prayed for and have come to love that person who wounded you. What happens if he or she hurts you again? Can you still love that person and pray for him or her? It doesn't matter if the person who wounded you has changed or refuses to change, your responsibility and duty is to continue to pray for them and allow God to love them through you. Remember, only God can change his or her heart, not you and not me.

_____

_____

_____

_____

What Was Meant for Evil, God Meant for Good

> But Joseph said to them, "Don't be afraid. Am I in the place of
> God? You intended to harm me, but God intended it for good
> to accomplish what is now being done, the saving of many
> lives." Genesis 50:19–20

I have heard this saying: "What was meant for evil, God meant for
good." I never really knew what that meant. After I started explor-
ing the command to love my mother and pray for her, God started
showing me what that little phrase meant. He took me to the story
of Joseph in Genesis. He showed me what Joseph had gone through
at the hands of his own flesh and blood.

God did not mean for my brother and me to suffer the evil that
came upon us at the hands of our mother. He gave my brother and
me to my parents as gifts from Him and as a reward for their love for
each other. My mother took a beautiful thing and poured a cup of
wickedness upon us that gave new meaning to the word cruelty. The
mental scars left behind are still healing, and I will never really get
rid of the horrific memories or some of the intense fears and feelings
that I feel from time to time. Don't get me wrong here; God has
done some miraculous healing in my body, heart, mind, and spirit,
and I am a completely different person today than I was even five
years ago. However, I know that I will never truly get rid of all the
scars until I am in the presence of my Lord.

An example of lingering scars is this: To this day, when someone drives up unannounced in my driveway, I start shaking and get defensive in a fearful manner. My adrenalin kicks in and it takes me hours to calm down even after the person leaves. It could be an innocent UPS driver or a friend who has come to call who didn't call before arriving in my driveway. That is one of the reasons we ask all people to please call before they come over and not just drop in.

I am still working on these fears and I hope that one day I will be like every other person and not have to be fearful when someone drives up my driveway unannounced. You would not believe the criticism I have been subjected to because of this fear. I have had people tell me to "get over it," that I am being paranoid and even crazy. I know I am not paranoid, nor am I crazy. I have a deep-seated fear of people showing up unannounced at my home and it is a direct result of the abuse I suffered at the hands of my mother, both as a child and into my adult years. According to my counselor, it is a direct result of the post-traumatic stress syndrome I suffered as a result of the abuse.

The question now becomes how can God take such a battered, bruised, and broken child and turn the evil that was done to her and turn it into something good? Good question. That is exactly what I wondered too. How could any good come out of what I went through? God says, "Stick with Me, kid, and I will show you." Uh oh! Be careful what you pray for! I am not sure I want to know. The real question was, "What are you going to require of me now, Lord?" Here comes another story of how God started to use my past experience for good.

I started working for a judicial office. My job was to help people who committed misdemeanors pay their debt to society. I began to see people—lots of them! Sometimes I would see twenty different people in one day. I got to know these people and I had the opportunity of learning a little bit about them and their history.

Then one day it happened. A woman wandered into my office and we got to talking. She had been abused and I was able to completely identify with her and share with her the love of Christ. Sadly, had I not gone through the abuse I went through, I would not have been able to understand what this woman had been through, and I certainly wouldn't have been able to plant a seed and show her the love of Jesus. What was meant for evil, God can turn into good. Now, did God have me go through all that abuse just so I could help that one woman? I don't think so. I do think that this woman was simply the tip of the iceberg for the people that God would have me reach with my experience, testimony, and love.

I know that the evil abuse you and I suffered was not part of God's original plan. I know that satan is alive and well and prowls around like a roaring lion looking for someone to devour. At any given moment, we are either listening to and obeying God or we are listening to and obeying satan. There are no two ways about it. Beloved, I want you to hear me here. The evil that was done to us was from the evil one of this world and not of God.

There is evil in this world, and Jesus Himself said that we would have trouble in this life, but we are to take heart because He (Jesus) has overcome the world. I don't understand why God allows bad things to happen. I don't understand why God would allow a mother to scar the gift—a beautiful little child—that was given to her by God. I won't know until I get to heaven and ask God personally.

The big *"but"* to the above is that when evil does happen to us, God can take that hurt and pain that we give to Him and He can use it for His glory. Don't turn this around. God does not like it when we are abused! He allows people freedom of choice; they must choose between right and wrong, good and evil, and God is the ultimate judge. Because of my abuse, because I allowed God to come in and heal me, showing me the way to forgiveness, and tenderly and lovingly showing me how to forgive, pray for, and love my tormentor, I am able to pass along not only my experience of the horrific events, but the forgiveness and healing as well.

I was not able to show this love until I got on the other side of the hate, anger, and pain. God can now use my testimony to help others, maybe even you, to forgive those who wound and abuse. In fact, that is the point of this book. I will say it again; I am not writing this book to focus on my abuse or my abuser, but rather to point the way to the only One who can heal our wounds, help us forgive our abuser, and use our horrific experience to help others do the same.

After you forgive your abuser, God can lead you to people who suffered the same abuse as you did. He can lead you to those who have not forgiven that person who abused them. God wants to heal the brokenhearted and the wounded. He will put you in circumstances and bring people to you that you can identify with. It is a trickle-down effect and it all leads to one thing: pointing the way to Jesus Christ as Lord and Savior and the healer and lover of our souls.

Think about this for just a minute. Who are you more drawn to? The person who has experienced the same problem that you have faced or the person who has no idea what you are going through? For me, my heart naturally gravitates toward those who are victims of abuse or who have been downtrodden by the world. Why? Because I can identify with them; I know their pain, and I have dealt with some of the same feelings and issues that they are dealing with or have dealt with.

Here is a perfect story to accompany the meaning of the above. We have a Great Pyrenees. Her name is Casey, and she came to us from a very abusive situation. We found out that she likes to run after deer! We have another dog that sticks close to home and can be trusted off a leash. Not true for Casey Roo. About a month or so after we got her, she decided to run after a deer and was on the run for thirty days. Long story short, after a lot of tracking, over 200 signs posted, and praying, she was found. We were very fortunate and got her back safe and sound. Needless to say, she is not allowed off her leash when she goes outside anymore.

Anyway, the point of the story is this: Since that incident, we have seen signs that someone put up saying that his dog was missing. We haven't seen the missing dog, but my husband made the comment that he should contact the person looking for their dog to see if he got the dog back. We could completely identify with that person and what he was feeling and maybe we could lend a little comfort to his life at this difficult time. The point is that we can identify with people who have gone through similar situations that we, ourselves, have gone through.

I have talked a lot in this book about you and I being the victim, but I would like to take a minute to talk to the person who is reading this who was both the abused and abuser. While I don't condone your acts of evil toward one of God's children, I do understand that you are repeating sin and are probably in a sin cycle. Just because you have carried on the sin cycle and you, yourself, have wounded someone, it is not too late to turn from your sin. No matter what you have done or the pride that is welled up within you; you can always call out to God; humble yourself, repent, and ask for forgiveness. He will hear you and He will forgive you. God doesn't take away the consequences, only the guilt of your actions. He can restore the years the locusts have eaten. You still have to deal with the consequences of the past, but God can forgive you. I would encourage you to humble yourself and fall on your knees before Almighty God. Give up your pride; tell Him you have sinned and have wounded others. He will forgive you. He will change your heart.

If you are still abusing someone, stop it! If you are gossiping about someone, stop it! Stop doing the things you know are hurting another person. You won't be able to stop by yourself, you need God's help. I must warn you to be prepared though; He may very well ask you to go and make the wrongs you have done right. That is part of the price you will have to pay. Wouldn't you rather pay the price here and maybe have people look upon you in disgrace than to have Almighty God looking at you with disgrace at the judgment seat of Christ? For there you will not be able to hide or make excuses or justifications about what you have done. There are always consequences for our sins. The question becomes would you rather deal with that punishment here on earth or in front of Almighty God? The choice is yours.

━━━━━━━━━━

Have you ever met people who have not dealt with their pain from abuse? They are bitter people who are angry and so nasty you can feel the pain that they try so hard to cover up deep inside. I have a cousin like this. He is so wounded that he looks at the world through eyes that tell him that everyone is out to get him and no one is to be trusted. He grew up with an alcoholic, abusive father. He doesn't know the love of the Lord and has kept all that hate and anger for himself. How sad, when he could let it go and feel a peace and love that surpasses all human understanding. Just between me and you, I think he is angry at God for allowing this to happen to him.

How about you? Can you identify with my cousin? Are you harboring feelings of bitterness, anger, and resentment? I was there at one point too. I questioned God on why I had to go through the abuse. Why did he put me with this woman as my mother? I look at other mother-daughter relationships that have love and are supporting of each other and ask God, "Why couldn't I have a relationship like that?"

━━━━━━━━━━

I am reminded of another Bible character named Job who questioned God when satan was allowed to rock his world. Job lost everything except his life, home, and wife. Job lost all his flocks and herds, his children, his money, and even his health; when Job started demanding and challenging God, He gave him quite the tongue-lashing. I choose to just tell God that I don't understand and let Him be in control.

━━━━━━━━━━

I will never understand why God allows bad things to happen. I don't understand why satan is the ruler of this world. He is a liar and a thief, and his only mission on this earth is to kill, rob, and destroy from God's children and His creation. I don't know if you know this or not, but when God created lucifer, He created him as a beautiful angel. Unfortunately, satan, or the devil, wanted to be worshiped and praised just like our Holy God. Jesus was tempted and asked by satan to bow down and worship him and he would give Jesus all the kingdoms of this earth. Jesus, the true living Son of God, shot back with the Word of God and told satan to go away from Him and quoted Scripture, saying, "Worship the Lord Your God and serve Him only!" You can check out the story for yourself in Matthew 4.

I want you to know that if you are reading this book, it is not by accident. God loves you and He knows what you have been through. If you are one that has suffered at the hands of another in an evil act of abuse, please know that you are not alone. You have not suffered in vain, nor have you suffered alone. God was with you as He was with me. He will comfort you and will bring justice to those who hurt you. My heart breaks for you, and I have shed tears for you and have prayed for you. It doesn't matter that I don't know you. God has allowed me to feel your pain, and I have prayed for you. You have my love and prayers. I would point you to Jesus Christ, for He is the only One who can truly heal and help you.

I hope you understand that God never meant for you to be hurt by another person. Don't think you are alone in dealing with your feelings of anger and not understanding why God allowed this horrific horror to happen to you. Just know that God loves you and He knows your name and the number of hairs on your head. I don't even know how many hairs I have! Rest assured, God does and He loves every follicle, every cell, every blood vessel, everything. He made you and He loves you. No matter what you have been through, God can take that experience and turn it into something good for others to glean hope from. Trust Him. He knows your pain and your hurt. Trust in Jesus and He will heal you because what was meant for evil, God meant for good.

The whole point of this chapter is to tell you that what happened to me and, quite possibly to you, was evil and not of God. If you give up your hurt, bitterness, pain, embarrassment, shame, anger, and hate to God, He will take your horrible experience and make something good come out of it. Maybe you will be able to lead someone to Christ. Maybe God will call you to preach about your experience to others to help them forgive and surrender to the Holy will of God. You don't know how God can use your pain and shame for His glory, but He can use it and He will if you will allow Him to.

Let's review the facts:

1.   There is evil in this world. The fallen angel, satan, and his band of outlaw renegade demons are constantly attacking, tormenting, and tempting the children of God. We don't know why God would allow this. We are not God and we have to trust Him, as He is ultimately in control and no one and nothing can touch us without God allowing it. Again, we don't always understand, but God has a plan for each of us. Trust Him!

2.   The abuse you suffered at the hands of someone else was not of God. Yes, it was allowed, but God never meant for you or me to suffer like that. God calls us to forgive and step out of the way so that His justice can be done.

3.   If you will allow God to work in your heart and life, He can take the evil that was done to you and make something good come out of it. It may be that He would have you share your pain and anger with someone who has had a similar experience to draw them closer to Him. We have to remember that whatever God calls us to do with our experiences, it will be to glorify Him and His name and to draw His children closer to Him.

Questions to Ponder

1. Are you still angry and bitter toward God for the wounds you have suffered? Can you let them go? Can you trust in Him to heal your heart?

_____

_____

_____

_____

2. Have you carried on the abuse? Have you or are you abusing someone right now? If your answer is yes, you need to stop, now, immediately. You cannot know the scars you are leaving on that person's soul and you will have to answer for and pay a price for the abuse you inflict on others. Remember, God can forgive you and help you to change, but you have to make the effort and take the first step. There will be no sweeping anything under the rug; it will be exposed for the ugliness that it is. You will have to suffer consequences, but God loves you, will forgive you, and He will help you get through whatever it is He asks you to do.

_____

_____

_____

_____

I want to close this chapter with a prayer and I would ask that you pray with me:

Merciful, loving Father, I love you and praise you! Father, there is someone who is reading this right now who may have abused someone because he or she was abused. I would ask that You would work in his or her heart to bring about your purposes and will. Father, there is someone who can't let go of the anger and bitterness; someone is angry at You for allowing this horrific experience to touch his or her life; someone can't imagine how You could possibly take his or her broken situation and make anything good come out of it. Please remind us that You are in control and You have a purpose and a plan for each of our lives.

Jesus, I would ask that You bind up the brokenhearted, give freedom for the captives of hate, anger, pain, and release from darkness for the prisoners. All of these special children are Yours. You created every one of us and You love us because we are Your children. May Your hand of favor, blessing, and grace be upon us and may we live to serve you, Mighty King. We lift right now our pain, hurt, shame, and bitterness to You and ask that You heal our hurting, broken, and shattered hearts. In the only name that is above all names, Jesus Christ, our precious Lord and Savior, amen.

Abuse in the Workplace: Forgiveness Is the Key

A student is not above his teacher, nor a servant above his master. So do not be afraid of them. There is nothing concealed that will not be disclosed, or hidden that will not be made known.

Matthew 10:24, 26

As he stood over me and started talking, I was shaking inside. Could I type as fast as he could speak? What if my fingers faltered? What if I missed a word? I had to try. I typed exactly what he told me to type and then he asked me to read it back to him. I read back to him exactly word for word what he had said. "I didn't say that? Are you stupid? Can't you hear?" But I typed exactly what he said. I didn't understand. This went on for a year and half. I felt my heart pounding in my chest. I couldn't take it anymore. My face, arms, and body were covered in ugly hives that were red and swollen. My skin hurt and my heart ached. I called my husband and asked him to please come and get me: I was quitting. This was the first and last time I would ever quit a job without having another job lined up. Financial questions ran rampant through my mind as I contemplated whether I was doing the right thing or not.

He went into the meeting thinking they just wanted to review his worksheet to see how it was working out for him. He got to the meeting in a really good mood, sat down, and faced satan head-on. There they were. Three people being used by satan to totally destroy his confidence, attack his character, and destroy his self-esteem. What took place at this meeting was a verbal assault on my husband's character, mind, heart, and spirit. They accused him of not doing his job; they trumped up charges of not keeping the facilities clean all the time; they stated members of the congregation had complained about the condition of the buildings; they were angry that he didn't turn his worksheets in and account for every second of the day. They told him to straighten up or he would lose his job. They put him on indefinite probation, stating they could fire him at any time for any reason if they were not happy with this work.

Funny thing, this was the first time in the four years he had been with the church that complaints had arisen. Could it be a coincidence that my husband's main boss was a man who was married to a woman who was close friends with and worked with his mother-in-law, my mother? I think not! After all, his mother-in-law strongly suggested to him that he look for another job. We didn't think much of the comment at the time, not until things started adding up and falling into place. It was another attempt from my mother to destroy my husband and myself.

After picking up the pace and working double time, he asked his boss if he could have a vote of confidence as to his progress and if he had met their expectations. The boss gave him a big vote of confidence and said he was doing a great job! This was one week prior to the next meeting.

The next meeting came around and he went into the meeting feeling good and confident that he had done what they had asked. He went into the meeting, sat down, and the first words he heard were, "We have decided to terminate your job." There was silence for about ten seconds and then in a laughing, joking manner he heard, "But we have decided not today. We told you that you had to comply to the letter!" This mind torture sent his blood pressure sky high, the adrenalin coursed through his veins, his face turned red, and his heart was pounding so hard in his chest he felt he would have a heart attack. After more demoralizing verbal attacks, they sent him on his way with a new date with the executioner.

All of this mental torture caused a loss of appetite, loss of sleep, irritability, frustrated anger, elevated blood pressure, gallbladder pain attacks, diarrhea, severe migraine headaches, loss of sex drive, depression, despair, and brought both of us to the brink of a nervous breakdown. I list these symptoms because I want you to know what stress of that magnitude can do to the body, mind, and spirit.

For the record, my husband had never had a black mark on any job review and his performance evaluations had always been exemplary. He had always been told that he was a hard worker, was always on time, rarely called in sick or for any other reason, went over and above the call of duty to help others out, and performed his job to the best of his ability. After these meetings with these people, he was feeling really horrible about himself. He lost his confidence, self-esteem, and self-worth. He felt useless, unloved, uncared for, and not wanted.

That very weekend, he ran into a former boss of his who was unsaved, ungodly, and very much in the secular worldview. This former boss had no knowledge of what was happening to him at his current job when he made the following comment: "I wish we could work together again. When we worked together, you did the job of two to three people." A little light came into his eyes. There was the briefest sparkle before his eyes grayed over again with depression and despair.

These are two examples of abuse in the workplace. There are countless stories like this all over the world. Some are worse than others, but it all comes down to people in power abusing their power and tormenting the workers under their control. The first example was a true story that happened to me when I worked for an attorney as a legal secretary, and the second story is the true story that happened to my husband when he was the custodian and caretaker of the surrounding grounds at our former church.

God is so good. In both situations, God provided for our every need while we waited for Him to open the next door. We did not want for food and our bills got paid. It was tight and we had to budget our money very carefully, but God provided what we needed when we needed it at exactly the right time. We were faithful to God as well, as we continued to tithe and give what He prompted us to give. Sometimes I questioned God because He was asking us to give out of our poverty in an act of trust. We did and He was faithful to provide everything we needed at just the right time.

Just as God gives gifts of children to parents and entrusts those parents not to abuse those precious gifts, so He also gives companies, businesses, corporations, and even churches gifts in the form of employees to care for and to perform certain duties and tasks. Do you think God is happy when He sees His children being abused in the workplace? Not anymore than when He sees His children being abused by parents, teachers, or other people.

If you have been abused in a workplace environment, take heart and know that what these people have done to you, me, and others will be brought before Almighty God, and they will have to answer to God Himself for their treatment toward all of us. Well, that is comforting when I die, but what do we do with the anger and pain in the meantime? I am so glad you asked! I would love to show you what we did.

We cried a lot, prayed together, and sought God's help in the matter. We were scared on the surface but had such a peace deep down that everything would be okay if we would just trust and obey. Well, that was easy for God to say because He can see the past, present, and future of the big picture. He can see everything that is in front of us that we cannot see. This was not very comforting to us. We were hurting, wounded beyond comprehension, and angry.

God started speaking to us through a Christian radio station, various sermons we would watch on TV, and then would send people into our lives to give us a hug or a word of encouragement. The message we received loud and clear was this: "I know you are going through a trial and it is painful. Keep praying and trusting Me (God). Keep your faith; get your house, finances, and bodies in order/shape. I am with you in this storm. Remember that you are not fighting against flesh and blood, but against the evil one of this world. (Uh oh! Here it comes!) I want you to forgive those who have wounded you and step away so that I can bring about justice."

I knew it! Forgive them! Anyone who knows me knows that I sometimes growl. I give a *grrrrr* when I am not happy with something. So what exactly did we think of forgiving those persons in charge of our paychecks who dangled them over our heads like a carrot? You got it! *Grrrrrrr.* I was growling.

———————————

My husband was wrestling with God, and God did an amazing thing! Remember the story of Jacob when he wrestled with God in Genesis and God touched his hip and Jacob went through the rest of his life with a limp? Well, God touched my husband's hip and it started hurting. Then He touched his leg and the pain went from the hip to the thigh and then to the knee. Was there anything medically wrong with him? No. He wrestled with God and lost. Case closed. It was shortly after that experience that we started going back to church after a five-week lay off. We didn't go back to the church where my husband was working, but we did find a church and, surprisingly, we found many friends of ours who had previously defected from our old church. My husband doesn't walk with a limp; God healed him, but the message was clear. No more wrestling with God; we needed to forgive the people who hurt us. We went through fire and storm, standing up against people who wounded us deeply and wrestling with God over forgiving these people.

———————————

You can be sure that after you have prayed and told God that you have forgiven the person who has hurt you, He will test you in your forgiveness. Through gritted teeth, we forgave the people who hurt us in the workplace. Then it happened. A very dear lady who we had adopted as a surrogate grandmother passed away. My husband, at that time, was still on staff at the church. Nobody bothered to tell him of her passing until five days after the fact. His bosses knew how much this woman meant to my husband and me. They knew that we would want to learn of her passing. How disrespectful, cruel, and inconsiderate to learn five days after her death that she had passed away! This hurt us deeply.

At the little memorial service and luncheon they held for her, only the pastor and my husband from the staff bothered to stay for the memorial service. The other staff members left right after they had eaten lunch. My husband's heart broke into many pieces once again. He was mortified and devastated at the actions and disrespect of his fellow co-workers. He thought they would have shown more respect for the passing of an elder of the church. Once again, we faced another situation in which we had to forgive people who hurt us.

One thing that we have found is that it is easy to forgive when you fully realize that God is in control and He will hand out justice. The people who have hurt others will absolutely have to give an account to God Himself for their ugly thoughts, words, and deeds. Take heart! Jesus has overcome the world! He is King of kings and Lord of lords and He reigns! This knowledge is really the only way we were able to forgive our tormentors. When God asks us to forgive, what He is really asking us to do is step aside and not take revenge or justice into our own hands, but leave room for Him to work. We don't always like the way He works and sometimes we think our plans are better than His: this is pride. God said that vengeance is His and not ours.

It is so easy to lash out at those who hurt us. Think about your workplace experience. When someone says something that stings, you want to be quick with a comeback that will equal that same sting toward that person. Stop at that point. Don't do it! That is taking revenge. I know it is hard. Sometimes our tongues are quicker than our minds and definitely quicker than our hearts. If we would just stop and think about the words that were said and then either go back and ask the person what he or she meant by that comment or simply smile and walk away, I wonder what would happen.

One thing my mother taught me that I use to this day is this: "Smile all the time, because when you smile, no one knows what you are up to or what you are thinking." I do this on a regular basis. I remember one particular moment in time when I did this. I wish you could have been there to see it! Since I like stories and you do too, I will share this one with you.

I was working at a judicial branch office, and I was working around lots of secular people who did not know the Lord. One of the gals in the upper office was always trying to make me angry or get me riled with her vulgar language and repeated taking the Lord's name in vain. One day, she made a horrific comment directed toward me and my faith in Jesus. Ouch! I stopped and smiled. I looked at her, and smiling, I told her I liked the blouse she was wearing. I told her to have a good day and walked back to my lower level office.

I wish you could have seen the look on her face! It was a combination of stunned awe and disbelief. Here this woman had just slammed my faith and put down my precious Savior to my face and I came back with a smile and a compliment and never acknowledged her blaspheme. You know, at the instant that those horrific words came out of her mouth, I was angry. I was hurt for my Lord, but then a still, small voice deep inside my heart said, "I love you and I love this woman. Show her my love. She will have to answer to Me for what she has said. This is not your battle; it's Mine. I can defend Myself, so show her My love for her." Wow! I wish that gal could have heard Jesus's voice. I think she really needed to know that He loved her, so I showed her. I smiled and gave her a compliment and walked away. That's forgiveness and grace in action.

Workplace abuse has got to be one of the worst types of abuse out there. The problem is the at-will employee clause that many, if not most, states have adopted. This is totally unfair to the employee. The at-will clause states that an employer can fire an employee at any time for any reason, thereby totally devastating the home finances and, sometimes, future survival of the employee. On the flipside of the at-will clause is that the employee can walk out on the employer at any time for any reason.

Take a very close look at this at-will clause. Who benefits more: the employer or employee? The answer is obvious: the employer. If the employee walks out on the employer, chances are his or her position will only be vacant for a few weeks and the employer is inconvenienced without any real loss or hardship. If the employer decides to fire an employee, that employer is jeopardizing the very livelihood and survival of the employee.

I hear some of you saying, "Well, that is why we have unemployment benefits." True enough, but unemployment benefits are usually one-third of the employee's paychecks. So if the employee is a single mom living paycheck to paycheck and barely paying the bills and feeding herself and her child and she loses her job, how do unemployment benefits help? Now you have a single mom who was barely getting by and has to get by with even less. What does she cut out? Does she not pay the electric and have no electricity? Does she not pay the rent and not have a place to live? How about cutting back on food? She was probably living on macaroni and cheese and soup before she lost her job.

Now, I can't possibly complain about something like being an at-will employee if I didn't have a suggested solution. Take a look at the situation from the Lord's point of view. The Lord loves both the employer and employee. He would not want to see either one of them hurting or suffering financially or living in poverty. Did you catch that? The Lord does not want to see either the employer or employee suffering or hurting. When we are the boss, we are held to a higher standard. We have been entrusted with a life in the form of a person to care for and provide a living for. God demands that we are kind to our employees or those under our control. God tells us to speak the truth in love and to treat others as you would want to be treated.

For the employees' part, God expects us to work for our employers as if we were (which we really are) working for Him. He expects the employee to give 110 percent on the job and treat the job as if it were our own business.

The above being said, in an ideal workplace environment, you would have a boss who was kind and considerate of his or her workers. The boss would compliment the work or speak the truth in love when there was a mistake or a different way of doing things. The boss would pay the employee over and above what is expected and provide health insurance and other benefits to show the employee that he or she is valued more as a human being rather than just a lowly worker. The boss would never gossip about the employee to other co-workers, would reprimand all gossiping, would not allow vulgar language in the workplace that would include taking the Lord's name in vain, and would treat the employees as family instead of workers.

For the employees' part, they would give an honest, full day's work to their employer. They would go above and beyond the call of duty to help the boss to run the office, department, store, company, business, or corporation smoothly and with honesty and integrity. The employee would not take things from the business that did not belong to them, not take advantage of personal phone calls, refrain from gossiping about co-workers, customers, or others who frequent the business, and stay off the Internet for personal interests. The employee would also be honest about documenting lunch hours and break times, being careful not to abuse the time given in good faith.

That would be the ideal situation, and my thinking is if all bosses and employees would treat the other as they would their personal friends, this world would be a better place to work and live in. However, I know the reality of the workplace environment.

Let's go back to the at-will clause and the suggested solution. If I owned a business and had employees, I would set up a checklist disciplinary form and have all employees sign it along with the immediate boss. This checklist would outline the reasons for immediate termination of the job clearly and succinctly. The checklist would then define unacceptable behavior and a short list of disciplinary action steps to be taken prior to termination of the job.

Then I would redefine the term at-will employee. If the employee did not commit a crime or violent act toward another co-worker and the boss really doesn't have a good reason for firing the employee, I would enforce the following: The employee would be notified that he or she is simply not working out in the current position. The employee would then be given a grace period for finding alternate employment. If the employee does not find work within this grace period, he or she would receive an additional two weeks pay and he or she would be terminated as an employee. Since the employee knows that he or she will be terminated regardless of whether he or she finds a job, it would be the intent of the additional two-weeks worth of pay to get over the waiting period for the unemployment benefits to kick in.

If there is an employee who wishes to quit, he or she should give the employer a two- to four-week notice and offer to help train someone new. Many times, employees who are not happy in their job simply quit without giving the employer an explanation. I think this is a mistake. I think the employee should give the reason or reasons for leaving the job. I want to be perfectly clear when I state that the employee should give a reason. This is not a license to rip the employer up and down and point out all the mistakes of the company. The employee should express the issues in a loving, kind, and gentle manner. That is hard to do when you are angry and frustrated. My suggestion would be to take a few days of personal or vacation time and formulate your reasons on paper and then sit down with the boss when tempers have cooled down and you are in a better frame of mind. By providing the employer with the reason you are quitting, you could help the employer and provide valuable information for correcting future problems. I know many times neither the employee nor the employer really care about the reason, but we are not thinking from a worldly point of view, but from God's point of view. He told us to love one another. Both employers and employees should always remember one thing: they are not working for the other's benefit, but they are working exclusively for God.

═══════════

When my husband was enduring the horrific mind torture from his bosses, he would go to work every day and say, "Okay, God. Here I am to work for You." He would not give those bozos the satisfaction of sloughing off because he was hurt or wounded. He kept his priorities in order and realized that he would have to give God an account of his actions if he decided to do a poor job because he was hurt or because he wanted to retaliate for the pain they caused him. He simply refused to stoop to their level and kept doing the same wonderful job he had always done for them.

He knew the accusations that were hurled at him were not true. He went back to his Bible and read what God thought about him. God said he was His son and He loved him very much and was counting on him not to allow his flesh and humanness to interfere in the Lord's work. He gained new strength, wisdom, and insight into what God thought of him and did not buy into the lies that were brought against him. He pressed on toward the goal and kept his eyes focused on Jesus Christ. The way in which my husband handled this horrific situation shows how much he has grown. Even five years ago, he would have thrown up his hands, said a few choice words, and walked out. This did not happen. He hung in there and continued to turn the other cheek every time he was slapped.

═══════════

For those of us who are born-again Christians, we have a very unique role. Have you ever stopped to think that God has placed us in difficult job situations to lead others to Christ? Make no mistake; God has placed you in your current situation for a reason and He has a plan. We can't always see that plan or know what it is especially when we are working with people who are less than kind to us. It just may be that God has placed us in those situations to show the love of God.

Remember my story of the gal who was always trying to make me angry? I knew she didn't know the Lord. Jesus told me the words she said were painful to hear, and yes, they were an attack on me, but He asked me to show her His love. I did. That was a seed. Now God can take that seed and build on it. I don't know if this woman will ever come to accept Jesus as her personal Savior, but I pray for her and I planted all the seeds God gave me to sow; some of them were hard to plant because I was hurt by her words, but I obeyed and planted them anyway, regardless of her response. She could tell me all day that she hated me and that I am nothing but a Bible-thumping blowhard. I shook my feathers, praised the Lord, and smiled and gave her a compliment with all the love and sincerity God gave me.

Whether we are dealing with family, employers, co-workers, or total strangers, the underlying theme is the same. People wound people by their words and deeds because we live in a sin-filled, fallen world. No one is perfect, and there is no such thing as the perfect relationship. We can come close, but we will always have some strife and disagreement if we are around other people long enough. We cannot know what a perfect relationship looks like until we get to heaven and are in the presence of our heavenly Father God. Even the best relationships will end up wounding us from time to time. It is only when we repent of our sins against one another, ask for forgiveness, and give forgiveness that we are on the right path that leads to wonderful and everlasting relationships.

I know this sounds like pie in the sky, love, and flowers. I realize sometimes the hurts and wounds go very deep and it is very difficult to follow Christ and forgive, but He does not ask us to forgive; He commands us to forgive. Jesus does not always allow us to forget, but He equips and commands us to forgive and then we are to move on or forward always pressing toward the goal of heaven.

As with any relationship, if you are in a physically or mentally abusive relationship, I would strongly suggest you remove yourself from that situation and seek help immediately. You don't have to put up with physical abuse, nor do you have to live under mental abuse. God would not expect you to stay in an abusive relationship either.

Remember my story in the beginning of this chapter about the attorney I worked for? Well, I found out later after I quit, he went home and beat up his wife. Had I not had my husband there with me when I stated I was quitting, I know in my heart of hearts that he would have physically abused me as well. As it was, my boss's face turned a deep blood red and I could almost see smoke coming from his eyes and ears! The medical doctor I had spoken with later confirmed that had I stayed in that abusive situation much longer, I would either have had a nervous breakdown or a heart attack. The power of stress; don't ever underestimate it! It can literally destroy the body and break it down to the point of illness and even a serious disease like cancer or even death.

Before I wrap up this chapter, I want to ask one question to the employers of this world: Do you allow your Christian employees to share the gospel of Jesus Christ with your customers and other co-workers? If not, shame on you! The Bible states that Jesus commanded us to go into all the word and share the gospel with the lost and hurting of this world. He did not say, "If you feel like it." Nor did He say, "I suggest you share My Word." No! He commanded us to go into all the world and share the gospel about Jesus Christ being the only way, truth and light—no one comes to the Father except through Jesus.

Don't try to tell me about "separation of church and state." This is a lie straight from hell itself! Did you know that "separation of church and state" language is not in the Constitution or the Declaration of Independence or any other founding documents of this nation? Do the research yourself if you don't believe me. In fact, I have done it for you.

The First Amendment to the Constitution of the United States: "Congress shall make no law respecting an establishment of religion, or prohibiting the free exercise thereof; or abridging the freedom of speech, or of the press; or the right of the people peaceably to assemble, and to petition the Government for a redress of grievances."

The phrase "separation of church and state" is not mentioned in the Congressional Record from June 7 to September 25, 1789. This is the period that documents the months of discussions and debates of the ninety men who framed the First Amendment! Had separation been the intent of the First Amendment, it would stand to reason and would seem logical that the phrase would have been mentioned at least once, right? But no! It is not mentioned at all!

Unfortunately, radicals who have their own agendas have long been trying to rewrite the Constitution by making the First Amendment say something it simply doesn't. In contrast, the Declaration of Independence contains four references to God: God as the Creator and the source of liberty ("all men are endowed by their Creator with unalienable rights"), God the law giver ("law of nature and of nature's God"), God the ultimate judge ("the Supreme Judge of the World"), and God as the King above all earthly rulers, as the Sovereign ("Divine Providence").

Our founding fathers did not want any one religion to govern the peoples of this country. They wanted the people to come to Christ on their own and not be ordered or told to do so. That is what is meant by separation of church and state: don't force your religion on others; allow them to come on their own. It was never meant to prevent people from sharing the gospel of Jesus Christ.

If you allow your employees to share their testimonies and the truth of the gospel of Jesus with others, they will not be hurting your business, but rather they will improve business! Think about it. Would you rather have employees who share their testimonies and the gospel of Jesus Christ with others and improve the atmosphere in your business or would you rather have a bunch of unsaved angry people working for you who will do more harm with their ugly attitudes than good? The choice is yours; I think it is clear.

Let's review the facts:

1. Workplace abuse is more common than we think. There are literally thousands of workers each day who are either physically and/or mentally abused by their employers. They are overworked and underpaid, they take a lot of heat if the job is not done to the employer's expectations, and somehow the wages simply don't measure up to all the problems that come with the job.

2. We live in a fallen world, and there are no perfect people. No relationship is going to be without heartache and pain from time to time. This is just a fact of this fallen sin-filled world we live in. Take heart! Jesus is in control and in charge, and He can deliver you from your situation or at the very least give you the strength to go and work another day. Ask Him for wisdom, grace, and strength. When we pray to God, did you know that He does not necessarily change our circumstances or the people around us, but He changes us? He changes our perspective and ways of handling difficult situations, so His glory and love can shine through us and be a beacon of light to the lost of this world.

3. God loves both the employer and employee equally. He hurts when we hurt, and He sees our suffering. Because of the fallen state of this world, we can rest assured that this is not the life that the Lord had originally ordained for us. He has a far better plan for us. We need to have faith and trust and then watch for the doors to open.

Questions to Ponder

1. Are you in an abusive situation at work? Can you lay down your feelings toward those who are hurting you and rise above their immaturity with grace, forgiveness, and love? Your answer should be: not alone I can't. Apart from God, we can do nothing, but with God, all things are possible, even the seemingly impossible, like getting along with those who hurt us in the workplace.

_____

_____

_____

_____

2. Are you an employer? How do you treat your employees? Do you set expectations that are not attainable for them? Are you kind? Do you compliment their work or just give negative feedback when they make a mistake? Are you upholding the righteousness of God or do you have your own agenda? If you are an employer now, then at some point in your life you must have been an employee. How did you expect your boss to treat you? Go and do likewise, for God says to treat others as we would like to be treated.

_____

_____

_____

_____

3. How is your performance on the job? Do you give 110 percent every day? Do you take little things that no one will miss home with you? That is stealing. If you surf the Internet during working hours, that is also stealing. This is stealing your boss's time and getting paid for not working. Don't get me wrong here. You are probably entitled to breaks and a lunch hour. You don't have to be a slave, but you do have to be a good steward with the time that God has given you to do the work for your boss. So many times I see people standing around talking for ten, twenty, thirty minutes at a time about anything and everything except work-related issues. The boss may not always be around to make sure you are working—that is trust on his or her part. What you have to remember is that you are not working for your boss; you are working for God, and He is always watching and taking notes!

_____

_____

_____

_____

If you are currently in a difficult working situation, let me pray for you:

> Father God, I just want to thank You for providing for us, Your children. Father, You provide us with jobs that pay our bills and put food on our tables, and we are so very grateful to You. Sometimes, Father, we are placed in working situations where other people wound us and hurt us deeply. Sometimes the job does not pay as well as we were led to believe or the benefits are not sufficient to provide for our families. I would ask You right now, Father, to bless the one who is reading this and is struggling in a job. Please provide a way out for this person or change the hearts of the co-workers so that the treatment would become better and more manageable. You don't always take away our burdens and You don't always remove us from difficult working conditions. You leave us where we are at so that we can come to You for comfort and strength and quite possibly to lead others to Your Son, Jesus Christ. You require that we shine for You in these places if for no other reason than to give hope and point the way to salvation for the lost and hurting. Please give us Your wisdom and strength as we press on in our jobs. Help us to endure the abuse from co-workers and bosses as they mistreat us with harshness and not Your love and grace. We ask that You would lead us by Your Spirit and guide us into Your truth. Please help us see Your plan for our lives. We lift all this to You and ask it in the name of Jesus. Amen.

Forgiving Wounds Inflicted by a Church Family

Therefore this is what the LORD, The God of Israel, says to the shepherds who tend my people: "Because you have scattered my flock and driven them away and have not bestowed care on them, I will bestow punishment on you for the evil you have done," declares the LORD. "I myself will gather the remnant of my flock out of all the countries where I have driven them and will bring them back to their pasture, where they will be fruitful and increase in number."

Jeremiah 23:2–3

What happens when your pastor fails? What happens when you start getting the cold shoulder from members of the congregation and you don't know why? What do you do when you realize your pastor has lied to the congregation, shattering your faith and trust in the church? What happens when the people of the church have turned the church into a fashion show social gathering instead of a place of worship? Pretty tough questions, but this is exactly what happened to my husband and me at our little church where we renewed our vows, came to salvation in Christ, became members, were baptized, and served faithfully for many years. Before I get to the end, let me start at the beginning.

I do not want to put down or taint any denomination, so I will refrain from mentioning the denomination of our former little church. Just because a church is of a certain denomination does not mean that all churches of that denomination are corrupt or inadequate. It was not the denomination that caused the trouble, but rather it was the fact that our pastor had withheld important information about the reality of homosexual partners receiving part of the congregation's tithes and offerings as benefits and did not tell the truth about supporting homosexual domestic partners with our tithes! It was also the fact that our pastor did not stick up for my husband and me when the lies, slander, and gossip started circulating through the church about us.

In the beginning, I was searching for a church home and family. I felt disconnected and wanted to join a church where I felt welcomed and accepted for who I was and not for what I wore or how social I was. When I walked into our small-town church for the first time, I felt loved and welcomed. After a while, my husband started attending with me and he felt that same love and welcoming spirit. For five years we called this little church our home, and we loved not only our church but our church family as well.

Our little church started growing in numbers, and we were soon over four hundred members and attendees. What a blessing! We were both very involved in our little church. We played the usher roles, the greeter roles, and various other roles that allowed us to get closer to our church family and serve God in ways we could not even imagine. It was truly wonderful! We made lifelong friends and were really starting to gel as a church family.

Then it happened. We had a bright, energetic young man who joined our church and became our youth pastor. After a couple of years, he learned that part of our tithes and offerings were going to support a gay minister and his domestic partner! As you can imagine, he was mortified and outraged and realized that this issue had to be addressed by the pastor and the truth must be told. It wasn't until much later that we learned the truth of what took place. Our youth pastor ended up leaving the church and the state with his family. The church shunned him and the pastor gave several sermons relating to how we were to allow God to judge what is right and wrong and how we had no control over where our monies were spent. He stated this situation really did not affect our little church because it was a district problem. After all, the domestic partnership between two men was not taking place in our little church. Sadly, that was not the point.

The truth was that the pastor refused to deal with the truth and the issue of homosexuality and then further refused to answer any questions by the congregation relating to the subject. Many of the church members got together and asked the pastor if they could use the church to discuss this situation amongst themselves; again the pastor refused.

Red flags started going up when the pastor stated he would refuse any kind of transfer to another church. He was staying at this little church and had no intention of being led to another church, regardless of whether God or the powers that be in the district church wanted him to leave. I know that pastors get called from time to time to pastor different churches, so what was wrong with him transferring if that was what was required of him?

More red flags started going up when children were allowed to run banshee through the sanctuary without regard to people who wished to pray at the foot of the cross or who simply wanted to pray quietly in their seats. The sanctuary became a social gathering with people laughing loudly and talking about all things not related to God or worship of Him. When we started to correct the children and tell them not to run and scream in the sanctuary and attempted to maintain a quiet and reverent atmosphere, we were the ones who got into trouble by the parents. Apparently, it was okay for children to run and scream in a sanctuary and be disrespectful in God's house.

The final red flags went up when going to worship became a fashion show. Can I tell you something? God doesn't care what you wear when you worship Him. He is not looking down on His people in churches and pointing out the people who are in the designer dresses and suits. He does not care if you wear a tie or a blouse or if you come in your slippers and pajamas!

My husband and I were not rich, but rather we were poor church mice that didn't have expensive clothes to wear. We were wearing clothes we had purchased ten to twenty years ago or that were handed down from friends or purchased at garage sales. If God truly cared about what we wore, He would not have created us naked as jaybirds in the beginning!

———

Remember what happened when man fell from the grace of God? After Adam and Eve had eaten the forbidden fruit, God stitched animal skins together for them to cover their nakedness. If you want the truth, God created us naked and wanted us to worship Him naked, bearing all before Him as our Father. It was because of the fall of man that we recognized our nakedness and were shamed. God did not find shame in His creation; we did!

———

Let me get back to the fall of our little church. People started leaving in droves. They were deeply wounded and angry. I believe it was not the only issue of supporting homosexual partnership benefits that hurt us so badly, but the fact that the pastor lied about where our tithes and offerings were going or what they were supporting, and he kept it hidden and refused to deal with the questions the congregation had. The pastor had preached in a sermon that he did not care how many people left the church; he said even if five people were left, he would still be at the same church preaching.

At the same time of this sermon by our pastor, I had just heard a sermon by Dr. David Jeremiah where he stated that if pastors did not care how many people attended the church, then there were probably not a lot of people attending that church. Coincidence? I think not! Our little church went from over four hundred members and attendees to less than 170 within a seven-month time frame.

———

One day we walked into our little church and had no idea it would be our last time. We were greeted at the door fair enough, but as we neared the sanctuary, we started seeing the cold stares of people; no one came up to us to welcome us or even say hello. We felt shunned and we had no idea why. As we went into the sanctuary, there were kids running and screaming, and my heart was breaking. I wanted so desperately to go up to the altar and kneel and pray. I needed strength, as we were going through a very tumultuous time in our lives, and I really needed my heavenly Father, and I felt the need to go to the altar. There was loud laughing and talking about anything and everything that had nothing to do with God or attending Sunday service. My heart was breaking and the tears started to flow without promise of stopping. Our little church had become nothing more than a social gathering and romper room for undisciplined children.

Sadly, that was our last Sunday in our little church. We had given so much of our lives to that church and to the people. We felt that we were being abandoned yet again by the people we called family. If our own pastor wouldn't talk to us or even be honest with us, then who could we trust?

As if we needed more confirmation that God was pulling us away from this church, about a couple of weeks prior to attending our last Sunday service, I attended my regular growth group Bible study. I was mortified and appalled when our growth group leader attempted to lead us in a stint of yoga! She stated that yoga was a Hindu practice and it was good for the body and encouraged us to meditate and hum like the Hindus do in their worship! Let's review a fact here: Hindu religion worships cows and they believe you don't go to heaven or hell when you die but rather are reincarnated! That is idolatry, and God says to stay away from all religious practices that could lead you astray and away from God. Deuteronomy 18:9: states: "When you enter the land the Lord your God is giving you, do not learn to imitate the detestable ways of the nations there."

Many people in today's culture see no problem with practicing yoga, astrology, mysticism, sorcery, or other spiritual-related practices not of the one true, living God. There is an old saying that rings true every time and it goes like this: "Birds of a feather flock together." When you practice things of another religion that does not worship the one true God of Abraham, Isaac, and Jacob, you are messing with fire and can be led astray from what is true and righteous. One thing leads to another, and before you know it, you are involved in a cult or with people who have no regard for God but make up their own rituals and practices and think they are worshiping God when in reality they are worshiping either themselves, the earth around them, or satan.

> Therefore watch yourselves very carefully, so that you do not become corrupt and make for yourselves an idol, an image of any shape, whether formed like a man or a woman, or like any animal on earth or any bird that flies in the air, or like any creature that moves along the ground or any fish in the waters below.
> Deuteronomy 4:15–18

Stay away! In fact, we are told by Jesus Himself when we are faced with temptation, we are to run away hard and fast in the other direction. Run from temptation. Don't think you can play with fire and not get burned. Don't think you can dabble in yoga, sorcery, horoscopes, astrology, mediums, spiritualists, psychics, or any other type of mystical practice and not be affected and led astray.

Our growth group leader started practicing yoga and then, to make matters worse, she confessed that she did not believe that hell existed. She stated that she believed God was a loving God and would never send anyone to hell. That was the last growth group I attended in our little church. God opened my eyes wide and let me see the reality of what I was listening to and absorbing from my growth group leader. I had a choice. I could either shrug it off as nothing or listen to God's Word and flee for my very life or rather my very eternal life. I ran hard and fast and vowed not to return to that place. If I have a chance to obey and follow God and believe what He tells me as opposed to what common man tells me, I will take God and His Word every time. I serve God and not man. I don't care what people think of me and I am not here to please people. There are only two people whose opinions I value: Jesus Christ, my Lord and Savior, and my husband. Outside of that, I really don't care what people think or say about me as long as I am justified in the sight of Jesus or my husband. And with that, I will now step down off my soapbox and continue on with the story.

It was five weeks before we would attend another church. We would watch sermons on television and worship and praise God in our own ways throughout the days and weeks, but I felt that something was missing. I missed worshiping with other believers. I missed singing with a band in worship and praising my King, Jesus. I missed the fellowship, but we were so wounded that we dare not trust anyone. We got up the courage and decided to start attending a church some of our friends had defected to upon leaving our little church. We saw many people we once fellowshipped with and felt like we might be at home again.

We started going every Sunday, and the worship was wonderful and the fellowship was good too. We went into the sanctuary and there were no screaming kids running around. The lights were dim, and the mood was soft and one of reverence and respect. We heard little whispers here and there, but what we saw and heard was total respect and awe for the Sabbath and for Almighty God. We felt God's presence strong and true.

Later, I found out they were forming an Open Hearts program and they had a softball team! We love to play softball! Yes, it was really starting to look and feel like home. Some of the faces were different, some were familiar, but all were friendly and welcoming and it didn't matter if you were in jeans and T-shirt or a suit and tie. No one really seemed to care what you were wearing or if all your hairs were all in the right places.

Well, all that was wonderful, but there were wounds to be dealt with. We were still hurting, and we didn't want to talk to or associate with anyone who was still attending our former little church. Many of our friends who had defected spoke of being terribly wounded and hurt. As people started to leave one by one, the horror stories started to surface and be shared. No one still attending the little church bothered to call anyone who had left to find out why they hadn't been in church; it seemed as if no one cared.

The pastor from our former little church had actually yelled at a couple who we knew were his best friends and stated he no longer wanted to associate with them or talk to them. Similar stories started to surface about how the pastor and his wife had said ugly words to people once believed to be their friends; horrible acts were committed against former parishioners—people being shunned, excluded, or gossiped about. Friendships were being destroyed, hearts were being broken, and, in some cases, spiritual death had taken place in some members. John 10:10: "The thief comes only to steal and kill and destroy; I have come that they may have life, and have it to the full."

The word *destroy* can also mean divide. What better way to destroy people than to divide their church family? One of the ways that satan tries to destroy us is through our relationships with one another. If we are united, we are strong; if we are divided, we are weak. God created us as relational beings. We were created to relate with one another and have relationships; we need each other. If we are divided, then there is hurt, strife, pain, and mistrust. Pride creeps in and then we have people taking sides, judging each other, and the gossip wheel starts turning.

We had to take a look at the pain in our hearts over this situation and forgive the people who wounded us. That was hard. God loves the people who hurt us as much as He loves us. He was not happy with the way they were acting, but He still loved them as His children. In our humanness, we can't understand how God can love someone who has wounded us so deeply. We don't like that person, nor do we wish to be around such people, but God still loves them! How can that be?

For the answer, we have to ask ourselves if we created the person who wounded us. No. If you are a parent and your child says something that terribly wounds you, do you stop loving that child? No, of course not. Now magnify that love by trillions and you might have a small comprehension of how much God loves His creation. Think about the last time you said some ugly words that wounded your spouse or a friend or even your child. Do you think that person stopped loving you? Probably not, but I will guarantee you there is now a wound where those ugly words penetrated.

Do you know where a lot of pain and wounding comes from? From not apologizing. If our pastor would have gotten up and apologized for not being honest and humbled himself in front of his congregation and admitted his humanness, I don't think our little church would have been so divided. I think there would have been forgiveness and grace. There would be consequences to pay, but those consequences could be easily dealt with and handled properly if humbleness and not pride ruled the day.

Pride is such an ugly barrier between God and us. I am just as guilty of harboring pride as anyone. I make it a regular practice to examine all of my thoughts, words, and deeds to make sure I am not harboring pride in any fashion, but it still creeps in from time to time, and it is usually closely accompanied by selfishness. Those two seem to go hand in hand. I am not saying that all wounding comes from a place of not saying your sorry, but a lot of it does. If someone physically wounded you, I don't think saying you're sorry would hold much weight, but a lot of wounding that we do verbally can be healed far faster by simply coming clean with our sin and apologizing to those we have offended or hurt.

God has started showing us what He wants His church to look like, and, let me tell you, friend, it has nothing to do with being Catholic, Lutheran, Methodist, Baptist, or any other Christian denomination. The church of Christ should be just that—a group of people who have accepted Jesus as their personal Lord and Savior, who have repented (turned away) of their sins, and who live for Him, obeying His commands. After all, we are told in the Bible that we will bow down and worship the King of kings and Lord of lords, every tribe and tongue. Does that sound like denominations and segregation to you? It does not sound like that to me. I believe that is how Jesus wants us to be; don't classify yourselves as Catholic or Baptist or whatever. We are all Christians. We believe in Jesus as our Lord and Savior, and we are to be united as one in Christ, for He is the Head of the church.

There are really only two groups of people in this world: those who are saved by Jesus Christ and those who are not. It is that simple and that uncomplicated. Either you are a follower of Jesus Christ or you are not and are bound for hell. I am sure I will catch a lot of flack for these statements, and I really don't care. If you have a problem with these statements, don't take it up with me, a simple instrument and humble servant of God; take it up with Him. He is the One who made the rules and stated that there is only one way to heaven, not me. Jesus is the One who said that He is the truth, the way, and the life and that no one comes to the Father except through Him.

I didn't make that up or decide one day that was going to be the new rule for getting into heaven. I read, I accepted, and I believed. I don't question God about the way in which he decides who goes to heaven and who doesn't, but if you feel the need to question Him on this, then go right ahead. He can take it. If you do decide to question God, I would like to remind you of King Nebuchadnezzar. He thought he was "the man" and questioned God on His authority over him and ended up eating grass like a cow and taking a shower in the dew of the morning until he came to his senses and gave God all the credit and glory He deserves. So if you want to question God on His authority and on whom He appoints as Savior of the World, then, by all means, be my guest. Personally, I have questions for God, but I do not wish to question His authority.

In fact, here are some of King Nebuchadnezzar's words after God got a hold of him.

All the peoples of the earth are regarded as nothing. He does as he pleases with the powers of heaven and the peoples of the earth. No one can hold back his hand or say to him: "What have you done?"

Daniel 4:35

Now, if this arrogant king can humble himself before Almighty God and realize that God does as He pleases and makes the rules, then who are we to question that authority? I was often fond of saying, "No matter how hard you shake your fist in God's face, He can squash you like a bug." We simply cannot comprehend how big our God is. We are as nothing to Him; even the tallest man at over nine feet tall, Goliath, was no match for God. Pretty impressive!

Just like anyone else, Christian people are not perfect. We mess up; we say things or omit things we shouldn't; we can fall from grace. If you look around and pay attention to the headlines, Christians are held to a higher standard than the people of the secular world. You never hear of women sleeping around with five or six different men at a time; however, when a pastor or reverend falls and gets caught in his sin, it makes the front pages of the newspapers and is among the top stories on the evening news. Why is that? Because people look at Christians differently and hold them to a higher standard. Also, when a Christian person sins, the rest of the world points fingers and claims that we are not as righteous as we pretend or claim to be.

What they don't realize is that we are human too, and we sin just like the rest of the world. We are not perfect. The only difference between Christians and the rest of the world is that we have accepted Jesus Christ as our personal Lord and Savior and He alone has washed away our sin by the shedding of His blood on the cross. That's it. Nothing flashy; no good works or deeds; no rules to uphold, just a simple belief that Jesus came to earth not to condemn the world, but to save it; to die for our sins by crucifixion; to be buried and rise back to life on the third day. We confess our sins to Him and He is good to forgive us our sins. It is because of His love for us that we seek to please Him by performing good works and following His rules, not because He is forcing us to or that we have rules to obey. God did not set up His commands so that we should be dour and never have any fun; He set them up for our own protection and safety.

I have to share this with you. I saw a bumper sticker on a car that is so true. It said, "The Ten Commandments are not multiple choice." Isn't that great? I laughed and laughed, but that is a very true statement and is so true! How many times do we say, "I don't murder; I don't steal; I would never cheat on my husband or wife, but I tell a lie every now and then or I covet my neighbor's brand new Lexus." We can't pick and choose which commands we will obey. In fact, God says that if we have broken one of the commands, then we are guilty of breaking all of them!

Repenting of sins and asking for forgiveness should be a daily ritual; we should all be in the practice of doing it every day. "Pick up your cross daily and follow Me," is what Jesus said. He didn't say, "Accept Me once; ask for forgiveness one time and all will be okay." No, He said, "Take up your cross *daily* and follow Me." If you don't think you need to repent on a daily basis, ask yourself when was the last time you told a little white lie or outright lied or performed the sin of omission. If your answer was like mine and you said, "I was fine until I got out of bed this morning and then words just started coming out or bad thoughts started coming in," then you have your answer about the need to repent on a daily basis. The day you do not commit one sin against Holy God is the day you don't need to repent and ask for forgiveness.

Christian men and women fall from grace too. We have to forgive those who have wounded us and move forward. You will not be able to do this on your own. The only way you will be able to forgive even a church family who has wounded you is to call upon the name of the Lord and ask for strength, wisdom, and also ask God to show you if you have hidden wickedness in your heart. It may be that though you have been wounded by your little church family, you may have contributed to that wounding in some way. Ask God to show you. Don't just point the finger and say, "You are a bad church or church family because this is what you did to me." Take a hard look at your own actions, thoughts, words, and deeds to make sure you did not help participate in the wrong behavior. There are always two sides to every story. Make sure that your story is right with God, and if it is not, you will need to repent and ask God to help you change as well as heal.

═══════════════════════

Before I wrap up this chapter, I want to say a few words about judging people in your church. If you see someone who is not a very social person, do not make the assumption about them that he or she is stuck up or think him or herself better than you. I just may be that person you are judging in this manner. I am quiet, do not socialize much, do not attend a lot of church functions, and am rather shy. I have been wounded so severely in the past that I don't trust others readily, and I can come across a bit standoffish. My husband is like this too. We both have been wounded to the very core and our hearts have been literally shattered by so many people so many times that our trust in humanity is almost nonexistent. It simply takes us a while to warm up and even trust people. However, once you have our trust, you have a loyal, honest friend for life.

God is working on us and showing us that this is really self-protection. Our guard is constantly up and to trust someone is literally a leap of blind faith. It is a struggle but one that we are working diligently on. Don't judge people by their outward appearances. You have no idea what is living under the surface, nor do you have any idea what the person you are judging has gone through. It just may be that the very person you are judging has seen horrors you can't possibly imagine or have ever lived through.

Believe it or not, people can shatter trust, respect, self-esteem, self-confidence, and love in another person by their words and deeds. Like I stated at the very beginning of this book, I am writing this book to help me to heal and not necessarily for you. If you are reading this book and have been helped by it, then praise the Lord! The reality is that I am writing to help heal my wounds, and if it helps you to heal yours, then God has touched your heart and I am glad for you.

———————

I know of some pastors who have abused their flock in a sexual manner. I will be very vague on this, because it happened to a very dear friend of mine and it so shattered her faith in the church that she has stayed away from attending any church. I don't know if she will ever again trust enough to join corporate worship, but I keep praying for her. She does not trust anyone who is a pastor or clergyman. I can only imagine the horror she went through.

Then there is the horrific behavior of certain Catholic priests who have sexually abused children. How do we deal with people who claim to follow God but do detestable things to other human beings for their own gratification? The reason I bring this up is because forgiveness in these situations does not come easily and the wounds are very deep and could actually have a negative impact on the faith of the person. This type of behavior comes directly from satan and has to be looked at as an attack on God Himself. What better way to remove people from the church and from following God than to allow shepherds of flocks to fail or fall miserably before the world?

———————

Sadly, my husband and I stopped attending the new church and family we thought we had found. We asked the pastor one Sunday if we would be taking communion soon, as we had not done so since we started attending this new church. The pastor's response so devastated us that we have not returned.

The pastor stated he would not be serving communion in his church because he didn't want to offend people who had not put their faith in Jesus Christ and went on to state that Holy Communion was offered at Wednesday worship. Are you kidding me? Really? Jesus stated to his disciples during the Last Supper before His crucifixion that the reason He broke bread and drank wine and shared it with them was so that we would do this in remembrance of Him and His sacrifice for us. Jesus died for us and our sins, and this pastor didn't want to offend anyone by practicing this remembrance? Jesus stated that if we are ashamed of Him before men (and this includes being afraid of offending people with the Gospel truth), then He will be ashamed us of before the Father. We have not been back to this church since, and to this day, we are church homeless.

We have gone back to watching our sermons on Sunday mornings, daily Scripture reading, and prayer. We know that someday God will lead us to a church family who is Bible-based and remembers the sacrifice Jesus made on the cross for our sins and isn't afraid of offending the secular humanists and the world by performing Holy Communion.

As I close out this chapter, I hope you realize that Christians are human too, and we are not perfect, and we do mess up, and we do sin. We are not above, nor are we below, any other human being on this planet. It doesn't matter where you go to church; all of us are susceptible to failure and we can all fall from grace. The good news is that if we repent of our sins, God is gracious to forgive us our sins and restore us to righteousness.

Let's review the facts:

1. Even the best pastor among us is prone to falling from grace. We are all human and will not succeed in our quest for perfection until we are reunited face-to-face with our Lord and Savior, Jesus Christ.

2. Don't put preachers, evangelists, reverends, or any other person on a pedestal and think that they are the be-all and end-all of your world. Listen to many different preachers and many different sermons and allow God to speak to your heart through each of them.

3. God will never go against His own Word. He will never say that homosexual relationships are accepted; He will never condone lying or cover up; and He will not condone His children following after other gods or practicing bogus rituals because it simply feels good and looks good to man. These are His words and not mine. I am not narrow-minded, nor am I a bigot. I despise the sin but love the person. If you know of someone who is in the chains of homosexuality, the bondage of lying, the sin of cover-up, or the practice of detestable ways to God, then pray for these people. Pray for God to open his or her blind eyes and unlock his or her deaf ears. Pray that the Holy Spirit would gently and lovingly guide him or her into all truth.

4. Men's ways and thoughts are not God's ways and thoughts. What seems right to a man can lead to destruction and a future in hell. My best advice to those who have been let down or wounded by a pastor or a godly person you looked up to is to attempt to confront that person with God's truth and then pray for them. You need to forgive the person who wounded you and realize that the person is human and is prone and susceptible to fail and fall from grace. Place all of your eggs in the hands of God, but don't put all of your eggs in one human basket to trust that they will teach you, without flaw, the Word of God.

Questions to Ponder

1. Have you been in a situation where you felt your faith being tested or shattered by a godly man or woman you trusted?

_____

_____

_____

_____

2. Have you forgiven those in pastoral positions that have hurt you? If not, forgive them so that you can heal and God can deal with them according to His justice. Depending on the severity of the wounds, you may have to seek Christian counseling to deal with the complexity of your pain. The bottom line is: Do not harbor these negative feelings; they will only bring you down and hurt you. Remember, when you fail to forgive someone who has wounded you, it is like drinking rat poison and hoping that the person who hurt you will die. The reality is that you are only hurting yourself and not the other person.

_____

_____

_____

_____

3. Do you listen to other sermons by other pastors or preachers who do not attend your church? My suggestion would be to find a good Christian radio station and start listening to its programming. Watch Christian television and pay attention to those pastors and preachers who speak at other churches around the country. Read books by different Christian authors to get different perspectives on various subjects. If your pastor is opposed to you listening to other preachers, run as far and as fast away from that person as you can. This is not a person who has God's will and your best interests at heart, but rather his own pride and gratification in his thinking that he is the best person to translate the Word of God and no one else is qualified. This is wrong.

———————————————————————

———————————————————————

———————————————————————

———————————————————————

If you have been wounded by a pastor or church family, I would like to pray for you:

Father God, I thank You for corporate worship and fellowship with other believers in Christ, Your Son. Thank You for the salvation that only Jesus can bring. Father, there are some who are reading this book who have been terribly wounded by their pastor or church family. I would ask that You would restore their trust in You, help them to forgive the one who has wounded them, and help them to find a church that You would have them worship in. I pray for the person who has been physically or sexually traumatized by a trusted pastor or preacher. You know those wounds and the scars of pain left behind by those vile acts of sin. Please touch the heart of that person right now and help them to heal and turn their anger into forgiveness. This is so very hard for us, Father, because we want to hurt and get back at the person who hurt us. Please forgive us for sinning in our anger. We ask for Your strength, wisdom, and guidance as we struggle to get through this thing called life. We lift all this to You and ask it in Jesus's name. Amen."

Time to Move on and Go Forward

I press on toward the goal to win the prize for which God has called me heavenward in Christ Jesus.

Philippians 3:14

It's time to move on; time to get going. While it is true that we have no idea what lies ahead, we can trust in God. I hope, by now, you have given up your hate, anger, shame, pain, bitterness, and all the other negative feelings you may have toward someone who has wounded you. This is excess baggage you do not need to carry around with you. All of those negative feelings just drag you down and keep you in bondage and chains.

I hope you have been able, through God's help, to forgive the person who wounded you and have surrendered him or her to the Lord. It's not easy, is it? No. In my own journey, there are still times when I have to forgive my mother again and again and again. I find the old hate trying to sneak in when I hear another lie or something else has gotten back to me that she has done or said. My anger burns deep within my heart and soul, but I have to fall on my knees and give it to God, lest the negative feelings eat me alive.

I have another story for you! What I want you to take away from this real-life situation is the fact that you may not be able to completely reconcile with the people who have wounded you. God may have changed you and done a great work in your life to bring about healing, but the people who wounded you may not have changed at all. I want you to know that is okay, and God does not force us to have relationships with those who have wounded us. If He allows the relationship to reconcile, great! However, God may very well have to do some very hard work in the person's life that has wounded you in an attempt to get his or her attention and help him or her to get on the road to change. Here is the story:

My mother had problems breathing on Father's Day and was driven to the hospital. She called me and told me what was going on and that she might have to have a pacemaker put in her heart to help regulate the beating of her heart. My own heart broke for her, and the Holy Spirit prompted me to go up to the hospital to see her. I thought that maybe enough time had passed and maybe God was going to do a healing work right there in her hospital room. I knew I was taking a huge risk by going to see her, as my father had forbade me in a letter to associate with the family (remember, I told you he kicked my husband and I out of the family). I prayed and asked God to forgive me for dishonoring my father, but my mother was in the hospital and I felt the need to see her.

I got to her hospital room and was not there two minutes when she started telling me I needed to cut my hair because it was far too long. Then she started making other controlling comments and barking orders at me. I knew she was glad to see me, but I also realized she had not changed and was still trying to control me and manipulate me to her ways. Tears filled my eyes, and when I think about it today, tears still flood my eyes. I was so disappointed. Hadn't she learned anything? Hadn't any of my letters gotten through to her? Why was she still treating me as if I was fourteen instead of a forty-something adult woman who was living her own life?

In passing conversation with her, I confided to her some of the issues I was dealing with at work and the trouble I had gotten into for sharing my faith and the testimony of Jesus Christ. She told me that I should not share my faith at work. I immediately rebuked her and told her that is not what Jesus tells us in the Bible. Jesus said to go into all the world and share our faith. He did not ask us if we wanted to; He did not say if you feel like it share your faith with others. No, Jesus said go into all the world and share your faith with the lost and hurting. I knew then that my mother was entangled in satan's grip and that was all the more reason to pray for her and, unfortunately, to stay away from her.

My point here is that my mother had not changed. God had done a great work in my life in allowing me to not only forgive my mother for abusing me but also to actually have loving feelings and compassion toward her. My mother refused to take responsibility for her words and deeds toward me and expected me to take all of the blame for the division of the family. This is simply not true, nor was it realistic.

I want to share one other thing with you regarding the visit with my mother. As you know, God works in very mysterious ways. For many years, actually, truth be known, up until I went to see my mother in the hospital that last time, I was very frightened of her. I would start shaking at the sound of her voice and to look upon her sent waves of fear, adrenalin, and anxiety coursing through my body. Remember, I told you of my fear of people stopping over unannounced? This fear was part of the fear that I had not dealt with and it had continued to be a burden for me.

As I walked into that hospital room, I didn't know what to expect, but I can tell you I had no fear! I was not afraid of her. That was strange. As I was driving home after our visit, the following thought came into my mind: "I had to show you how very weak and vulnerable your mother was so that you would stop being frightened of her." Wow! God had allowed me to see my mother in a very weak and vulnerable state so that I could see her humanness and realize that she no longer had power or control over me. What a revelation! I started crying and just melted before God, praising and thanking Him! I didn't have to be afraid anymore! I could stand up and speak the truth of God's Word and confront my mother with truth and love. I no longer had to allow my heart to be penetrated with her ugly words and I didn't have to be controlled by her, nor did I have to fear her anymore! Praise the Lord!

As I kept thinking about the way my mother tried to control me, even in a hospital room, anger tried to creep in and I tried to block it. You know what? It is okay to be angry. Even Jesus was angry when he saw the priests disrespecting His Father's house. The trick is not to sin in that anger. That means no retaliation, no revenge, no trying to get back and hurt them as much as you have been hurt, no using bad words or language, and no fighting. I was happy to realize that I had kept my tongue in check. I had not disrespected my mother, nor did I dishonor her. I simply spoke the truth—and here is the important part—in love! I spoke the truth in love; not with harsh words or an angry tone, but in love!

We must realize who it is we are really fighting against. Remember, it is not flesh and blood; it is the evil one of this world. The best advice that I can give you is to tell God all about your hurt and angry feelings. Tell Him how angry you are. Tell Him exactly how you feel—He can take it—He is a big God. He knows your pain; He knows how angry you are, and chances are, He is angry too. Not at you, at the act that was done to you and at the person who the act came through.

To help you move forward, I would encourage you to talk with a Christian counselor. Get with someone you can trust and share your feelings. A counselor can help you put things into perspective and can share God's heart with you. You are not going to heal over night. The damage that you have suffered is going to take a while to heal and God will have to work on your heart. He may have to prune you of some destructive people in your life. He may have to completely take away people in your life who are a bad influence on you. Don't be afraid. It is okay. Pruning hurts sometimes, but God will always reveal the reason to you, which brings me to another story.

This is not a funny story, but it does illustrate how God prunes us. After sending letter upon letter to my mother; I knew I wasn't getting through. There came a point when God said, "You need to walk away from this family and honor your father's wishes to not associate with them anymore." What? Walk away from the only biological family I have ever known? Are you sure, God? He was quite sure. He asked me to honor my father's wishes and not contact my family anymore. I felt strangely guilty about that and prayed about it. God was firm. I was not to contact them, but to simply walk away and honor my father's wishes of no contact. That was very hard to swallow. I prayed and asked God why.

I didn't get my answer until God asked me to write this book. All of my life, my mother never had anything good to say about any decision I made in my life. God knows the influence and impact my mother's words have on me. Had I shared with my mother that I was writing a book on forgiveness, she would have shot me down and given me a million reasons not to write this book. I probably would have gotten discouraged and would have given up without writing this book.

God has a plan to bring as many of His children back to Him as possible. I believe He will use this book to help others who have suffered abuse. Not just to help people forgive their abusers, but to actually help them come to love and pray for their tormenters and abusers; leading people to Christ. It is for His glory, not mine, that I write this book. My mother is ensnared by satan's pride and she would have continued to try to prevent me from sharing my story and ultimately leading others to forgiveness in Christ.

Remember what Jesus said to Peter after Jesus explained to His disciples that He had to be handed over to the Pharisees of that day to be crucified? Peter told Jesus that it would never be so, and Jesus said, "Get thee behind me, satan!" If Jesus had listened to Peter and had not gone to the cross and died the way He did, you and I would have no hope of salvation or spending eternity in heaven.

See how satan works? I am sure that Peter thought he was protecting his dear friend and Lord by saying he would not allow Jesus to be captured and die. In reality, satan was prompting Peter to attempt to protect Jesus because satan knew the plan and did not want you or I saved; but rather, he would love to see us in hell with him! You can read the account for yourself in the book of John in your Bible.

So God asked me to walk away. I trust Him to once again restore my family and I pray that there will be complete reconciliation and healing.

Please hear me again on this: I did not write this book to shame my mother or put the spotlight on my abuse. I wrote this book to point people to Jesus Christ—the only way to true salvation, healing, and forgiveness. It is my prayer that people who read my story would not focus on pointing fingers or say, "That poor girl." No! I am alive today and have a voice and it is all because of Jesus! He has healed me; He has taken away my guilt and shame; He is restoring what the locusts have taken away. I forget what is behind me and strain toward what is ahead. These are Paul's words in Philippians 3. He was abused, too, but he wrote letters not so people would feel sorry for him but to glorify Jesus and bring honor to our Holy God. That is my hope as well. I would like very much to hear that you have forgiven the person who hurt you and hear that you are a follower of Christ and that you now pray for the person who wounded you.

I would also encourage you to go through the *Breaking Free* Bible study by Beth Moore and get into an Open Hearts class. If your church does not offer these programs, I would encourage you to find a surrogate church to go through these two studies. You may even want to consider bringing these studies into your church. The *Breaking Free* Bible study you can go through by yourself, but the Open Hearts really needs to be with a group. These two resources are wonderful and have helped me tremendously. And then find a good friend, someone you can share your hurt and pain with, preferably someone who has gone through a similar experience as you. Find someone you can open your heart to and who will keep your confidence and hold you accountable when you drift into your old habits of hate and revenge.

Take it from someone who has been there; you will drift back, but you don't have to stay there. It is easy to drift back and want to blame. Why? Because you are still hurting and people who are hurting want to hurt others. Don't come down too hard on yourself. Recognize this for what it is, get back into God's Word, cry out to Him in repentance, and move forward.

Be very watchful during this time, because you will be very vulnerable and the enemy will try to creep in and start filling your head with all kinds of reasons why you are justified to take revenge and not forgive. From a worldly point of view, you are justified in taking revenge and not forgiving that person. After all, what he or she did to you was wrong, and by society's standards, that person needs to be punished. But God calls us to a higher standard. He calls us to model and be like His Son, Jesus Christ.

The question now becomes *how* do I move forward? The answer: slowly and on your knees. I talk a lot about forgiving those who hurt us and how we should give it to God, and it all sounds so simple. It has taken me about four years to heal and come to this point, and I still feel I have a way's to go. It does not happen overnight, and you will fall and you will fail at times. You will backslide, but the point I am trying to make here is don't give up! Keep pressing on toward the goal; hang in there with Jesus; take Him at His Word; He will heal you. It will take time. God loves you and I love you.

I will be praying for you as you read this book. I have prayed over this book and the people who will read it. I trust that God will lead those of you who truly need to learn how to forgive to this book as part of your healing therapy. I don't have all the answers. All I can do is share my experience with you and point the way to true healing and forgiveness. It is not the easy road; the path is very narrow and, at times, it feels like you are going to fall off the cliff, but take heart and hang on; your journey with the King is just beginning.

God says in His Word that He will never leave us or forsake us, and that is in spite of how wicked and evil we are! What comforting words! What words to live by! We are definitely fallen creatures, and we have a wicked selfish sin nature and God knows that, but He loves us in spite of our weaknesses and fleshly desires.

I want you to hear me on this, my friend. God loves the person who hurt you as much as He loves you. This was a very hard and bitter pill for me to swallow. How could God love a mother who abused her children? One reason, I believe, is because she was abused herself and does not know any better and by beating her children she is retaliating in some twisted, strange way against the very person who abused her. When people abuse other people, it is a sign of immaturity, inadequacy, and an inferiority complex. In order for my mother to feel in control, she has to control everything and everyone around her; that includes beating her children into complete submission with the aftereffects carrying on into adulthood.

––––––––––––––––––

Let me tell you how I have moved forward and that might help you to do the same. I have poured myself into the Bible, I have increased my prayer life, I now journal and write down thoughts and prayers on an almost daily basis, and I surround myself with positive, like-minded Christian friends. I have had to give up some relationships in my life because they were toxic to me and I was unevenly yoked with many of these people. I work very hard at walking away from gossip and trash-talking people. This is not always easy because the lure of gossip is always intriguing and helps to keep our minds focused on others instead of our sin and our relationship with God.

If I can encourage you in one thing, walk away from the gossip wheel. It is dangerous and it is a sin. When you allow yourself to talk of someone else's issues, weaknesses, or problems, you open a can of worms that could result in hurting others deeply. When you walk away from gossip and refuse to engage in the tearing down of someone else—be it a famous personality, a co-worker, family member, or stranger—you will be pouring water on that fire. If you walk away and do not engage, you are sending a clear message to the other participants: This is wrong, and I am not going to be a part of it, lest someone finds out about what was said and gets really hurt. Proverbs 26:20: "Without wood a fire goes out; without gossip a quarrel dies down."

Gossip brings others down, and it hurts people who are already hurting. Please don't gossip. My mother has done this to my husband and me, and we would have been reconciled long ago if she had just kept her mouth shut or only spoke the truth. It was no one's business to learn anything about my child abuse, but my mother had to lie and make herself look innocent, pretending to be the victim in this case in order to continue denying the truth and not taking responsibility for her actions. When you deflect the spotlight of truth away from you, then you can continue to live in the darkness and pretend all is well. It is a great trick that satan uses and many people fall for it.

———————————————

Another way I have moved on is by developing good habits and taking time out just for me. One of my problems was that I was running full tilt all the time and never took time to just sit and enjoy life. I like to crochet. I crochet all kinds of afghans, doilies, tablecloths, etc. I love to crochet and then give the finished product away. I make lots of graduation afghans and wedding tablecloths. I make doilies and theme afghans for Christmas. It keeps my hands busy, so I am not eating, and it relieves a lot of stress.

I also have picked up the habit of walking. I love to walk, and I walk on my treadmill and walk outside every chance I get. I especially love to walk in God's creation. The exercise is good for my body, and when I walk, I make sure I take along my Savior. He is always with me, but I find when I walk He is there to cheer me on or just listen to what I have to prattle on about. Walking and praying can speed up the healing process. We are encouraged to pray without ceasing in 1 Thessalonians.

———————————————

Can I jump off the track here and talk a little bit about praying without ceasing? For the longest time, I thought that praying without ceasing meant that I had to constantly be on my knees and pray a certain way. That is not what God meant by praying without ceasing. That is exactly the trouble the Pharisees got into. They made every rule and law God laid down a ritual and set the bar of expectation so high that praying became a duty rather than what it was truly meant to be—a conversation with your heavenly Creator! You can pray anywhere at anytime. God hears you! You don't always have to pray out loud; I rarely pray out loud, unless I am in my prayer room by myself. I find myself always talking to God. I pray in the car, the shower, when I walk, before I go to bed, and when I rise in the morning. I pray when I talk to other people! Whoa! A double conversation going on at the same time! I pray for people when I see them suffering or hurting.

Prayer can be as simple as saying, "God, please help!" or prayer can be lengthy as you pour your heart out before Him. To pray without ceasing simply means to have and keep a running conversation with God the Father. It takes time and practice, but now I can't even go five minutes without talking to God about something! No shock there. I am usually never at a loss for words! That was supposed to be funny and I hope you laughed a little.

Yet another way I have moved on is by saying, "I love you," to just about anyone and everyone I see and meet. I remember the first time I told my boss at my judicial job that I loved her. She was completely taken aback and did not know what to say or how to react. I had a good laugh over that one. What I mean by telling people that I love them is a deep respect and potential friendship that could be borne out of a caring, compassionate, and loving heart. I am not capable of loving anyone on my own; Jesus has to love them through me. I even told our car dealership representative that I loved him (with my husband present, I might add) and he smiled. It is like telling people you care about them.

Once you start telling people you care for them or you love them, this deep well starts bubbling up with love and mercy for others, and it helps in the healing process. It is not quite so scary to trust people when you are constantly telling them that you love them. You beat the negativity of judging others, and you let people know there is someone out there who really cares for them just as they are. It is a wonderful feeling. Try it!

Before I go on and potentially get myself in trouble here, let me explain the tone of voice for telling people you love them. You do have to be careful. You don't want to go around telling people of the opposite sex that you love them in a husky, deep voice full of temptation and innuendo. What I say is, "I just love you." I say it with a singsong voice and make it clear that the way in which I am saying it has absolutely no sexual connotation. What I want to convey is that I care about you; I am concerned for you; and I will pray for you. Remember, there are several ways to tell people you love them. There is a brotherly love that you can use with anyone. That is what I do; I treat people, regardless of their religious beliefs, like a brother or sister. I have a brotherly love for them and I tell them that I care for them and their well being.

Even Jesus asked Peter if he loved Him three times. "Do you love me, Peter?" Jesus asked. Peter said that he loved Him three times. Jesus and Peter loved each other as brothers. There was no sexual connotation from Jesus; He simply loved Peter and all of His disciples and you and me. You can check out Jesus's words in John 21.

═══════════════════════

Ultimately, what you will want to do is surround yourself with lots of love, mercy, and grace. Paul tells us to dwell on those things that are good and pleasing and not to dwell on the negative. This is easier said than done, especially if you have been wounded. Here is how I started thinking positively. There is no magic pill for being positive. I would read positive quotes and dwell on all the ways in which God had blessed me.

Count your blessings! Count the blessings we sometimes take for granted, like a roof over your head, food in your stomach, or the ability to brush your hair or put on your own clothes. These are huge blessings! How has God provided for you? Your life may not be perfect, and there may be a lot of hurt, but you do have blessings that have been given to you.

What I am talking about is taking a look around you and seeing the blessings that God has bestowed upon you. Dwell on those memories that make you smile and laugh. If there is something in your life that brings you down on a consistent basis, you need to get that something out of your life. If it is a person who is constantly putting you down, if possible, you need to distance yourself from that person.

Don't let anyone tell you that the abuse you suffered was in some way your fault or your own doing. This is a lie straight from hell. Another relative in our family tried to tell me that I was not a good girl when I was a child and I deserved all of the punishment my mother dished out. I understand why she said it. She was abused by her father and her husband and rather than take a look at her own pain and wounds, it was easier for her to justify my abuse so she wouldn't have to take a look at her own. It is so hard to be honest with ourselves and that is why God is the only One who can help us pull back the curtains and barriers we have put up in order to get a closer look at the wounds and how they have affected all areas of our lives.

That will be part of your moving on process: you will have to lift the barriers or bandages you have placed on your wounds in order to allow Jesus to come in and heal you. For example, my barriers were and still are, to some degree, to block painful memories. I relied on myself with total dependence upon myself: I didn't need anyone or anything. I also placed a layer of indifference or toughness around my heart. I don't hurt. I can handle it. I can take it. These were and are lies by the evil one. I was hurting deep down and I was growing a bitter root that had to be taken out. God told me that I could either pluck it out or He would have to remove it, but either way, it had to go. It was very painful to unwrap the layers that I had tried so diligently to cover up and protect. What I was doing, in reality, was fostering the hurt and pain and not eliminating it.

One thing that I didn't tell you is that it is okay to cry. I have cried rivers and oceans of tears. I have cried so much that I thought my eyes would permanently dry up. When we cry, we are releasing toxins that have been stored up in our bodies as a direct result of the wounds we have sustained at the hands of others. It doesn't matter if you are a man or a woman: cry. It is okay and no one will think you are weak for it, and if people put you down for crying, then run from them! They are not your friends. This was a very difficult thing for me to do, as we were not allowed to cry as children. I had a hard time crying in front of other people. God will heal that too.

Now I cry when I see others crying. Oh, I don't break down and start wailing, but tears flood my eyes and my heart goes out to them. This is what God calls replacing your hard heart with a sensitive one. For me, when I have those moments when I break down and do some serious crying, I raise my hands to God and I can almost feel His arms around me, holding me. The comfort and peace that floods my heart is almost overwhelming, and it helps me to know how much God truly loves me.

As I conclude this chapter, I hope you have gained some insight into how to move forward. Go slowly and don't try to force yourself to jump the steps that God will outline for you to take. Remember that you have been hurt and your wounds are probably very deep. The walls of concrete that you have surround your heart with are very thick and it will take the power of God, faith, and a strong belief in the truth to get you to break down those walls and open the wounds so Jesus can heal them. It won't be easy; nothing ever worth having is easy. Once you can slog through the muck of the pain, despair, depression, and anger, you will come out on the other side with a freshness and a newness you never thought possible. All of the unwrapping of the wounds will have been worth it. Trade in your ashes for beauty and your sadness for God's healing and anointing oil.

Let's review the facts:

1. Hopefully, by now, you have started to let go of some of the pain, hurt, and anger you have sustained at the hands of others. It won't be easy but it is possible. Allow Jesus to be your guide and trust Him.

2. Give yourself time and space to heal. It took me four years to get to this point, and God is still working on me. I haven't figured everything out, and I still struggle with continuous forgiving, and I have to fight the feelings of hatred that try to creep in from time to time, but I have a better grasp on how to handle those negative feelings.

3. It is okay to cry. You will need to grieve your pain and wounds. You will need to have a funeral for the pain you leave behind. So go ahead and cry and let it go.

4. And laugh! Find a funny movie or a funny book or listen to a Christian comedian. They always make me laugh! Just as you need to grieve, you need to laugh and get your endorphins going. It is part of the healing process and it works.

Questions to Ponder

1. So where are you now? Have you started allowing God to break down your barriers? Are you ready to open your heart to God and allow Him to come in and do a little heart surgery? I can't promise that it won't hurt; it probably will, but, my friend, it will be so worth it when you can finally unload all of that negative baggage and walk into the life God has prepared for you.

_____

_____

_____

_____

2. When was the last time you had a good cry fest? Get as many of the toxins out through your tears as you can. Crying all the time is not a good thing, but a good cry every now and then can really help you heal.

_____

_____

_____

_____

3. When was the last time you had a gut busting hearty laugh? Just as you need to cry, you need to laugh. Laughter can be good medicine and it helps the healing process.

———————————————————————

———————————————————————

———————————————————————

———————————————————————

Let's pray:

Father, God, thank You for the gifts of tears and laughter and for all the blessings You bestow upon us. Father, please forgive us when we take Your blessings for granted. Help us to take a look around us and see the blessings You have given us. Help us to move forward in our journey to forgive those who wound us. We know it is not going to be easy, but we have trust in You, and we are willing to follow Your plan for our lives. I ask You now to lift up my brother or sister who is reading this and help them to let go of the pain and move forward. I ask all this in the name of Jesus Christ, our Lord and Savior. Amen.

Conclusion and Summary

For God so loved the world that He gave his one and only Son (Jesus Christ) that whoever believes in Him shall not perish, but have eternal life. For God did not send His Son into the world to condemn the world, but to save the world through Him.

John 3:16–17

Jesus answered, "I am the way and the truth and the life. No one comes to the Father except through me."

John 14:6a

As I sit here with Sam the cat on my lap looking out the window at the birds on the feeder, I am wondering how I am going to wrap up this book. I could tell you that everything in your life will be okay and all you have to do is trust in God with love in your heart and flowers in your hair, but that is not going to help you in your pain that you feel now. Absolutely trust in God, for He is the only way that you will get through the pain of abuse, but your journey and your road will not be all fluff, flowers, and love. There are going to be a lot of tears as the layers are pulled back.

Remember when you were a kid and you fell down and scraped your knee or elbow or maybe scraped up your arm? Remember when you or someone else put a Band-Aid on the scrape and then had to pull it off to clean it or allow the air to get to it? Remember how that hurt? Ouch! I certainly do. Well, peeling back the layers of internal wounds is much like peeling back a Band-Aid from a scrape or cut. It hurts. It is very painful, and, if you are like me, you don't necessarily want to see what is under that covering. The scrape is even painful to look at, let alone allow air to touch it.

When you start peeling back the layers of your emotions and feelings and reveal the damage that has been done to your heart, mind, soul, and spirit, it is very hard to look at, let alone allow God to touch the hurt and help heal it. You need to allow the wound to breathe and the air to touch it in order for it to heal. It is the same way with your feelings and emotions. You need to let God touch the parts that are hurting and allow His grace, mercy, and love to be the salve that heals.

What do I mean by that? Well, don't fight God. When He prompts you to look deep into that well of pain, He wants to show you something about yourself and it may be ugly. When you can take a look at your pain, it will equip and enable you to empathize with and help others who have been in a similar situation as you. You will start to see patterns emerge that you never noticed before. Chances are there will be defense mechanisms that are so ingrained they are automatic when you sense danger or fear.

For example, God showed me that I had a tendency to allow people to walk all over me. I would listen to negative criticism about myself and just take it in and not bother to check to see if it was true. If it wasn't true, I wouldn't defend myself. I simply agreed with whatever someone told me and tried to change to please them. This is so wrong.

God has showed me how to speak the truth in love. Now when someone criticizes me, I check to see if it is valid and if it is not; I confront that person with facts in truth and love. The perfect example was the visit to my mother in the hospital. Remember, she told me I needed to cut my hair. Wrong answer! I don't need to cut my hair. I like my hair just the way it is, and I don't have to cut it to please her. So I politely told her, "No, Mom, I don't need to cut my hair." I didn't dishonor her, nor did I disrespect her. I simply stated there was no reason for me to cut my hair if I didn't want to, and that was my choice and not hers.

Another good example of this is when my mother, still in the hospital now, told me I was dishonoring her and my father by not communicating with them. I politely reminded my mother that my father had kicked both my husband and I out of the family and he requested that we no longer have contact with them. My mother denied this truth, and tried to use all kinds of excuses and justifications to prove otherwise. Everything from, "He didn't mean it," to "People do bad things under stress."

I gently and lovingly told my mother the truth of what my father had done and then told her that her response to the truth was not my issue or problem. I told her if she didn't believe me, to pray and ask God for the truth, wisdom, and discernment to distinguish right from wrong. I reminded her that the Holy Spirit would lead her into all truth if she was open to hearing it. Just that simple conversation was a huge example of how far I had grown in Christ in four short years. My heart was still heavy, but I felt pretty good about not blowing up at her and disrespecting her because she had made me angry.

———————————

It has taken me a long time to learn to stand up for myself. It doesn't come easy for me. I struggle with hurting people's feelings or saying the wrong thing. I don't think anyone likes confrontation, but sometimes you have to stand up for the truth and for what is right. You have certain God-given rights that you do not need to compromise or give away.

You have the right to wear your hair anyway you like. You have the right to share your faith with anyone you please. You have the right to praise God whenever and wherever you feel like it. You have the right to be treated fairly, with dignity and respect, no matter what situation you find yourself in, for we are to love others as we love ourselves. Don't allow other people to tell you who you should be; that is God's job. If He wants to change you; He will. My point in all this is to live free—free in Christ—because you are free. If the Son sets you free; you are free indeed!

———

Sometimes along the way, we can be wounded by others through their words and deeds. Some abuse is worse than others; some people have been wounded more than others. It is a choice as to how we are going to move forward after that abuse happens. We can choose to wallow in our hurt, wallow in the pain, wishing mishap, torture, or death upon the person who wounded us or we could throw a constant pity party for ourselves.

The other choice we have is to pick up all the pieces of our shattered heart and hand them to God and ask Him to restore, mold, mend, and heal us. He is the only One that will truly be able to heal your pain. You can go to counselors, pastors, watch advice TV, read advice books, or listen to advice radio stations and they may help a little bit as far as putting the pain into perspective, but they can't heal you. Only God can heal your wounds.

By the way, there is not a wound or a negative feeling that you are going through that God has not felt or gone through Himself. He was pierced for our transgressions, but by His wounds we are healed. Only by the blood of Jesus are we saved and only by His wounds are we healed. Let's just remember to be patient and not act like spoiled, rotten brats when we hand God our pain and wounds and ask Him to heal us. I get a picture of a little girl stomping her foot and shaking her fist at God and saying, "I want to be healed now! Right now! Take this pain away now!" No, God will take the pain away in His time and He will help you to grow and change in the midst of that pain.

There is a lesson to be learned here. We don't always understand the reason and we believe we don't deserve what has happened to us. We have to come to the truth that we live in a fallen world with fallen people and no one is perfect. That is not an excuse for the suffering you have gone through; it is just reality. Bad things happen to good people and it is not your fault.

I sit back and look upon my life and I can see the distant fading memories of a little girl who was once scared and scarred and battered and bruised. I can see the hurt and the pain, and somehow I know it is okay. The person who has hurt me can't hurt me anymore. I know what you are thinking. You say, "How can that be when your mother continues to lie and gossip and spread rumors about you?" It's simple really. I can either choose to listen to the lies and eventually believe them, or I can tell the person the truth when one of those lies comes to my ears. I don't have to get all self-righteous and stand on a soapbox proclaiming I was abused and the world should feel sorry for me. Not at all!

I take the opportunity to share my faith and explain that what that person has heard is simply not the truth. It is his or her decision to believe me or not; I don't care, because God knows my heart and He knows the truth and that is good enough for me. He defines my coming and going and He defines me as a person and as His daughter. I don't have to defend myself to anyone as long as I speak the absolute truth and know in my heart that what I have said is the truth and no exaggeration or lie has crept in. I have to answer to God and that keeps me honest.

Honestly, if you want to know the truth, I don't care what anyone thinks of me. Whoa! That sounded harsh. Not really. There are only two opinions that matters to me—God and my husband. I am not here to please man, but to serve my Lord and King, Jesus Christ.

When you can get to a point where you don't care what other people think of you, you are truly free to serve Christ. I know some people hate me; some people don't like me; some people don't like what I say. Oh well. I don't care! You know people didn't like Jesus either. In fact, they hated Him so much for speaking the truth of the Father that they tried to kill Him on a roman torture instrument called a cross. Death couldn't contain Him, hell couldn't stop him, and satan couldn't make Him change His mind about saving you and me. Jesus rose again three days later, defeating sin, death, hell, the grave, and satan in one swift blow!

I have seen more than my share of pain and suffering. I have lived through severe child abuse and lived to tell about it. I feel that I am stronger now than I was before. I know how to confront wrong thinking with truth and love. I know how to stand up for myself and I don't let insults or name calling bother me anymore. I have come a long way, baby!

On the flipside of that coin, I have learned how to have compassion for people, I have learned to love all people, and I have learned not to judge or gossip about others. I believe my journey is just getting started, and I am looking forward to what God has in store for me on the second leg of this journey.

If there is something I can give you to take away and hide in your heart, it would be this: God loves you. He created you. He knit you together by His hands in your mother's womb. He never meant for you to go through the pain and suffering you have gone through. I don't know why He allows people to hurt and wound each other. I don't know why He allowed me to go through all that I went through. I can tell you this: I am a stronger person with purpose and vision because of the experience. I would never wish abuse on anyone; the point here is that God can take the most shattered heart and heal it and then transform the abuse, pain, and evil that was done into good for someone else.

Jesus is the answer. Read the book of Isaiah in your Bible. Read the book of Job—you think you have troubles! I think the story of Job tops all of our hurts and shattered hearts combined! Read the book of John. In Isaiah, you will feel God's comfort for you. You will realize why Jesus was sent to earth and you will see a God who truly cares about you.

In the book of Job, you will realize that there existed another human being that didn't deserve to suffer so cruelly or horrifically. You will realize that no matter what you have gone through, it could have been worse. Job will help you appreciate the little things you have been blessed with. And in the book of John—so near and dear to my heart—you will learn that Jesus is God and you will learn of His great love and compassion for you. You will learn that Jesus died for you in your place and for your sins and transgressions.

For God so loved the world.

John 3:16

The thief comes only to steal, kill, and destroy.

John 10:10

I am the truth, the life, and the way; no man comes to the Father except through Me.

John 14:6

I have come to bind up the brokenhearted and to proclaim freedom for the captives.

Isaiah 61:1

I would encourage you to look up these passages of Scripture and read the whole chapters they are found in. I am sure they will speak to your heart as they have spoken to mine.

These scriptures are very near and dear to my heart. I honestly don't know where I would be without the Word of God as my lamp and prayer as my communication with the Holy Father. I think I would be in a loony bin somewhere strumming my bottom lip with my index finger and making inaudible noises! What are you laughing at? That's okay, I laughed at that word picture too. The point is I placed, with all of my trust, the pain, anger, hurt, hate, wounds, and shattered heart into the hands of Jesus and He took all of that and, over time, replaced it with joy, love, forgiveness, comfort, compassion, and mercy.

One other thing I want you to remember is that God never gives us more than we can handle. That is easy enough to say, but there have been times when I questioned God on this myself. At times, I felt like the hand of oppression was so heavy I was buckling under the weight and it felt like it would squish me like a bug, but somehow I was able to stand up and persevere.

When you pray for strength, God will give you strength. When you pray for wisdom, God will give you wisdom. Don't pray for death; that only makes God angry. I know; I prayed for death over and over and over again during the most painful parts of my journey. When I prayed and even begged for death, God took me to His Word, the Bible. He took me to Scripture that pointed out that He was not happy with me asking to die. He understood how I felt, but He had a purpose for me to fulfill on this earth, and if He took me home early, I wouldn't get all my work done that He has apportioned for me.

I can hear you thinking again: "What? You? Pray for death?" Oh yes. Yes indeed! You have to remember I am now on the other side of all the pain and hurt and my wounds are healing. However, there was a time when I was going through memory after painful memory recall; coming to the realization that my earthy father did not protect me, did not love me, or want me around; the whole family decided to take my mother at her word and shunned my husband and I; and compound all of that with living below the poverty line, Matthew losing his job at our former little church, losing our church family, and trying to make ends meet and not lose the only roof we had over our heads as a result.

When I look back at everything God has brought me through, I can't help but think of the footprints in the sand story. I honestly look back and see one set of footprints, and I know those aren't mine; they are too big! My feet are a size seven and a half, and these prints were gigantic! I know they were the Lord's feet and He was carrying me. Oh, what a sweet vision that is. Since our wonderful God is no respecter of persons, rest assured He will carry you, too, through the most painful and difficult times of your life. When your strength is gone and you are at your weakest, God becomes your strength.

I have talked about my past, about the abuse I suffered. I have talked about the abuse cycle and how we can keep the sin cycle going by treating people as we were treated. I have talked about generational sin and how that comes into play. I have talked a lot about healing and forgiveness, and now I think it is time to wrap up this book and let you get on with the business of healing your wounds and forgiving those who hurt you. So I will bring this book to a close with a few last-minute thoughts.

While I have used some humor in this book, I do not make light of abuse. I know the damaging effects it can have on the mind, body, and spirit. It is no laughing matter. Humor helps to heal, but please don't use humor to cover up your pain and attempt to forget about it. Pain and suffering that are hidden deep down inside always find a way to get out, either through physical illness, mental illness, or bitterness and ugly treatment of people. Don't bury your hurt; get it out in the open and deal with it. When you push your hurt and pain down and refuse to look at it, you are only hurting yourself. The sad thing is that pain and suffering have a way of surfacing at the most inconvenient and wrong times and can do severe damage to the people you really care about in your life.

Keep very open and fluid lines of communication going between you and God through his Son, Jesus Christ. I can't stress this enough. In fact, I have another story for you! I had to go to my boss at the judicial office I worked at about a co-worker who was completely incompetent in her job. This girl was strong-arming the people who had gotten into trouble and being rude and abrasive with them. It was just a matter of time before she would push someone over the edge with her nasty attitude and get hurt.

This was very difficult for me to do. At that time, I didn't have much confidence in myself, and I didn't want to look like a tattletale. But I knew I was doing the right thing and this gal had to be corrected if for no other reason than for her own safety. I wrote a ten-page report or memo outlining the issues and complaints against this co-worker. I didn't think I could give it to my boss. I was literally shaking and my stomach was so upset I couldn't eat. Finally, I put it in my boss's tray and went downstairs to the bathroom. I thought I would get sick and throw up. My legs were shaking so badly I could hardly walk and literally had to hang on to the walls.

In this bathroom, there was a little ledge and I placed my arms on this ledge and began to pray for strength. I cried out to God and told Him I knew I had done the right thing, but I was afraid of losing my job because I know my boss always took the side of this co-worker. As I was praying, in my mind's eye, I saw a very large figure in a white robe. He was big and strong and handsome, and he was coming toward me! I saw him reach out his hands and I literally felt him pick me up right there in the bathroom! He set my feet on what felt like solid ground and my legs immediately stopped shaking. He came to the front of me and wrapped his huge arms around me. I felt like I was totally engulfed in his robe and he just held me. When I looked up, he dried my tears and told me it was going to be okay. He helped me to stop crying and when I walked out of that bathroom, I was strong, solid, and had a confidence that was not mine.

I went back to my office and called a dear Christian friend of mine and told her what I had experienced. She immediately got very excited and said that God had sent either an angel or that Jesus Himself came to me to help strengthen me and comfort me. Wow! I started crying again! God is so amazing! God is so loving and caring and compassionate. He took this little lamb and put her back on solid ground, dried her tears, and told her it would be okay. He was there. He knew. He cared. He loved. He was with me!

It will be very important for you to pray without ceasing. Talk to God and tell Him everything! When you hurt, when you are angry, when you are happy, when you are excited, what makes you happy or cry—it doesn't matter! Tell Him! Talk to God and share every part of you with Him. That is what He longs for; that is why He created us—to be in relationship with Him.

How do you be in relationship with anyone? Communication! How did you get into a relationship with your spouse or your friends? Did it is just one day materialize? No. You started talking and talking and talking some more. Well, that is how we get into relationship with God.

We don't bring him a laundry list and say, "Um, now God, this is what I would like You to do for me today." No. How about starting out by thanking Him for what He has already given you. Make your petitions and requests at the end of your praise and worship. "Thank you, Father God, for this wonderful day! Thank you for the food on our table. Thank you for the roof over our head. Thank you for our children, pets, fish, mice, or whatever! Thank you!" The point is to be grateful to God for what you have. Don't take anything in your life for granted or God just may take away what you take for granted.

I wish for you happiness as you journey on to the goal that is living in eternity with Jesus Christ. My prayer is for you to be healed of your wounds and hurts and pain. I encourage you to lay down your hate, anger, pain, and revenge at the foot of the cross. You don't need that extra baggage weighing you down. I hope you have started down the road to forgiveness and healing. As I leave you, I would like to pray for you. You have my love, compassion, and empathy for your situation and the pain you have endured. You have God's love, faithfulness, forgiveness, mercy, grace, and trust. All you have to do is ask for it and He is gracious enough to give you all you need when you need it and He wants to give you so much more than you ever dreamed of asking Him for!

Father God, oh, merciful Father, how I love You! I want to thank You for taking the years of hurt and shame from me. I thank You for being on this journey with me every step of the way. Father, there is someone who is reading this book right now that is hurting and suffering. This person has suffered horrific treatment at the hands of another person. It would be my petition and request that You wrap that person in Your loving arms and heal his or her broken heart right now. Father, You have a wonderful way of untangling knots and messes we have either made or gotten ourselves into. We are sheep who are lost and easily led astray, but You are the Good Shepherd and You love Your little lambs.

I know You have felt the hurt and pain that my friend here is going through. Jesus, You suffered more than anyone and are alive to tell about it today! Praise be to Your name! I would ask You now to lead my new friend and help him or her into a beautiful relationship with You; heal his or her wounds; help him or her to break down the walls he or she has put up in an attempt to protect him or herself.

Father, I love You so much, and I praise You and thank You for being in my life and in the lives of these dear people who have dared to read my prattling words. May You use something of what I wrote to touch their hearts and allow them to forgive the people who have wounded them. You are faithful, God, and You love us. Thank you. I lift this person reading these words, their family and friends, and all of these prayers to you and ask it and claim it in the Name above all names, to the King of all kings, Jesus Christ. Amen.

Peace be with you always. May God grant you the desires of your heart that He has placed inside of you. May blessings and favor be upon you now and forever. Thank you for reading this book. I hope you got something out of it.

Finally, I believe in you! I believe you have the power to forgive those who hurt you and I believe you have the desire to live a life free of revenge, hurt, and pain. I am proud of you as well! I am proud to call you my friend and proud of you for starting a journey of healing and growth. I am proud of you for taking the first steps toward forgiveness.

Now, put the book down and call on a friend who will stick closer than a brother, one who will never leave you or forsake you. He is waiting to hear from you and the call is free! God bless you in your new journey! I look forward to seeing you in heaven if I don't meet you here on earth. Either way, I can't wait to hear your stories!

━━━━━━━━━━

Like I tell all my kids that God has given me, those He has brought into my life for some reason: "Take care and say your prayers! Eat all your organic vegetables, and try not to put the horse before the cart. The horse gets all tangled up in the reins and the cart goes around in circles, and go on now and live a life free from pain, hurt, revenge, anger, and strife! Thank you and God bless."